1234567
8910JQK

KQJ01 68
1234567

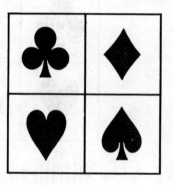

NEW CARD GAMES

by
Robert Abbott

BABEL

LEOPARD

AUCTION

VARIETY

METAMORPHOSIS

SWITCH

ELEUSIS

CONSTRUCTION

ULTIMA

FUNK & WAGNALLS / NEW YORK

First paperbound edition published 1968 by Funk &
Wagnalls, *A Division of* Reader's Digest Books, Inc.
Reprinted by arrangement with
Stein and Day/Publishers

Printed in the United States of America

The game Eleusis was introduced in the June 1959
Scientific American.
Ultima first appeared in the December 1962 *Recreational Mathematics Magazine* (now known as the
Journal of Recreational Mathematics). The game has
been substantially revised for this paperback edition.

TABLE OF CONTENTS

PREFACE

THERE ARE SOME SURPRISES IN STORE FOR YOU IN THIS BOOK.

There was a surprise for me in writing it. Inventing a game sometimes takes hundreds upon hundreds of hours, and the testing and refining of it in practice may take years of play. But getting a game down on paper so that the instructions will be clear and can be followed easily, I now know to be a task equivalent to taking a mountain and moving it, a shovelful at a time, to some other place. My effort will have been worth it, however, if readers everywhere now can share their enjoyment of these games with those people I have had a chance to teach personally, and who are now happily addicted to one or more of the games I have invented.

I have tried to incorporate in each game an element which would make it interesting — and, hopefully, even exciting — to a large number of players.

Babel, for instance, is designed to enable the players to imitate what brokers do on the floor of a stock exchange. It is also designed to overcome the handicap of some traditional games which can become boring when you sit around awaiting your turn. In *Babel,* it is always your turn, and there's no chance of getting bored. While *Babel* is fun with

5

just a few people, I've been host to *Babel* parties of from fifteen to forty people. It's one game everyone catches on to fast and once they learn how, they become addicted to it as I am.

Leopard is a fast-action game designed to give you every opportunity to sabotage your opponent.

Auction gives you the feeling of being at an auction, only you use your cards as money.

Variety has a real twist. There's no such thing as a bad hand — if you bid it shrewdly.

Metamorphosis you'll find to be a trick-taking game *unlike* any other.

Switch is a game in which four people keep switching partners every hand. It's very tricky, because a key element is picking the right partner, who won't always be your wife!

Eleusis is one of the very few games in which your powers of inductive reasoning are called upon. The dealer picks the governing rule of play and the rest of the players must figure out that rule in order to win.

Construction is a board game in which the board is built out of the cards *as you play*. Over the years, it's become a favorite of mine.

Ultima, or **Abbott's Ultima** as my game-playing friends call it, has been added to this book even though it's not a card game. The reason? It's the most complex game I've invented; Chess buffs may find it rivaling Chess in interest.

BEFORE YOU GET STARTED on any of these games, may I suggest that you read the whole game through. That first reading will give you the hang of the game as a whole.

On your second reading, with cards in hand, you can pick up the details. Experience has shown that this is by far the best way to learn a new game.

You'll notice that three of the games, *Babel, Auction,* and *Switch,* use Poker hands. Don't make the mistake of thinking that they are Poker variations. The important part of each game is not the ends (or card combinations) the players work for but the means by which cards are obtained or bids are made. It is these means that contain the basic conflict situation of the game. The distinguishing feature of Poker itself is not its hands but its system of betting. *Babel* and *Switch* are quite different from Poker. *Auction* has certain strategies in common with Poker, but others which are notably different. Some people will find one advantage in *Auction* over Poker: you don't have to play for stakes (that doesn't mean you can't wager on *Auction,* also; but the interest of the game doesn't depend on it).

I've used Poker hands in these games because most people know these hands and they're easy to remember. For those of you who may be unfamiliar with the Poker hands, however, they are explained in this book.

In closing, I want to wish you as much fun in playing these games as I've had in both inventing and playing them. Even if you find just one that becomes a standard with you and your friends, I'll feel my efforts justified.

—ROBERT ABBOTT

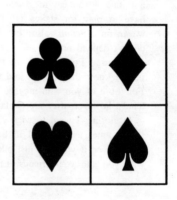

CHAPTER I

BABEL

**For
Three
to
Five
Players**

IF YOU'VE VISITED a stock or commodity trading exchange, or any free-wheeling market of buyers and sellers, you have some idea of what sparked my invention of Babel. As I stood at the rail of the visitors' gallery of the New York Stock Exchange one day, watching hundreds of grown men running, hollering, waving their arms, and, in the end, actually performing an important economic function, I saw that their activity could be thought of as a kind of game.

Economists have, in fact, analyzed the stock market in terms of a game in order to understand its underlying structure. But, I thought, would it be possible to create a game that captured the pure fun of the process?

9

Babel is my attempt to re-create the action at the Exchange. I can't promise that playing it will help to teach you how the nation's wealth is distributed. But you will experience an excitement similar to that which occurs in the bargaining situations on the floor of the Exchange.

More than that, Babel is a game in which everyone is participating at every moment. You never have to wait your turn; you are playing all the time. And what is more, the game works well for large groups. I have played it with as many as forty people, all of whom were running around, bidding like mad, and having the wildest time.

The standard game is for three, four, or five players and is described below. Following that is a version which can be played at a large party.

The Deal

USE a regular pack of fifty-two cards.

Deal ten cards to each player, and put the remainder of the pack face down as the stock pile.

Object of Game

THE OBJECT of the game is to get combinations of cards that score the greatest number of points. Scoring is based mainly on Poker hands and will be explained later. Although Babel makes use of these hands, it is quite unlike Poker, and you don't have to know Poker to play.

The Play

THE MAIN FEATURE of Babel is that the players try to get the cards they want by bargaining and trading with each other. First everyone is given a chance to arrange the cards in his hand. Then, after each has said he is ready, the bargaining and trading begin.

The players do not take turns; sometimes they haggle with one another; sometimes two players compete by bidding for a card held by a third; and often no one remembers who had first asked for what or offered what.

Here is an example of how the conversation might sound at one point:

"Does anyone have a nine?"

"I have a nine. Do you have a three of clubs to trade for it?"

"No."

"Do you have a four, a ten, or a queen?"

"No."

At this point a third player interrupts saying, "I have a queen. What will you give me for it?"

"A nine, a seven, or a two."

"Okay, I'll take your seven for my queen."

As you can see, there is no order to the play. The players should not wait for any transaction to be completed but should feel free to interrupt each other. And don't worry about talking while others are talking. In fact, anyone trying to be courteous is sure to lose.

As an added feature, two players may agree to trade a card "sight unseen." In this case each gives the other a card placed face down.

Two cards can be offered for one card.

The only restriction placed on the play is that a player may not look at another's hand nor show his own hand.

If the bargaining ever bogs down because the players, at the moment, have nothing to trade with each other, they may decide to draw from the stock pile. When someone proposes that they draw, the other players must agree to it before anyone may draw. After each player draws one card, the bargaining continues. *There is no discarding;* the players simply play with the larger hands.

Going Out

THE PLAY CONTINUES until one player goes out. All action must stop when a player says "I'm out," even if one player is about to hand a card to another. A player may go out if his hand contains any *two* of the following combinations: flush, full house, four of a kind, straight flush, or royal flush. (For those who aren't familiar with these Poker hands, they are explained in the table on page 14.) For example, if a player holds ♠7 ♣7 ♢7 ♢3 ♠3 ♠Q ♡Q ♢Q ♣Q ♠6, he may go out, since he has a full house and four of a kind. A player who holds ♡3-5-10-J-K ♠5-6-9-Q-K may also go out since he has two flushes.

A card that is used in one combination cannot also be used in the other.

Besides being able to go out with two of the above combinations, a player may also go out if he has one of the following combinations: double straight, double flush, double straight flush. These combinations are not borrowed from Poker as are the above. A double straight is any ten cards in numerical sequence, such as ♡3 ♠4 ♠5 ♢6 ♡7 ♣8 ♠9 ♣10 ♡J ♡Q; a double flush is ten cards of the same suit; and a double straight flush is ten cards of the same suit in sequence.

No bonus in scoring is given to the player who goes out.

Scoring

AFTER someone has gone out, each player figures his score by counting each combination he has as follows (again each card can be used in only one combination):

Pair	1
Three of a kind	3
Straight	5

Flush	7	
Full house	10	(a player may
Four of a kind	15	go out with
Straight flush	20	two of these)
Royal flush	21	

Double straight	30	(a player may
Double flush	40	go out with
Double straight flush	80	one of these)

If a player has more than ten cards, he must pick out the ten to be used for scoring.

The same hand can be scored in different ways; so a player should figure out which combinations give him the highest score. For example, the following ten cards, ♡6 ♡7 ♠8 ♡8 ♣8 ♣9 ♡10 ♠K ♡K ♣K, could be scored as:

♡6-7-8-10-K	flush	7
♠8 ♣8	pair	1
♠K ♣K	pair	1
♣9	no score	0
	total:	9

or as:

♠K ♡K ♣K ♠8 ♣8	full house	10
♡6 ♡7 ♡8 ♣9 ♡10	straight	5
	total:	15

The best score for this hand is therefore 15.

Each player's score is recorded, and a new hand is dealt by the player to the left of the dealer of the previous hand. A running total of each player's score is kept, and the first to reach 200 is the winner. If two or more players make 200 in the same hand, the one with the highest score is the winner.

Endplay

TOWARDS THE END of a game, when it is apparent that one player is clearly in the lead, the other players will often "team up" informally to try to keep the lead player from winning by ignoring him, denying him trades, etc. The lead player can fight back by offering one of the others some cards so tempting he cannot refuse to trade.

It is important to remember, especially towards the end of the game, that no player need accept an offer, or even answer an inquiry if he doesn't want to.

Card Combinations

THE FOLLOWING is an explanation of the card combinations:

Pair — two cards of the same number

Three of a kind — three cards of the same number

Straight — any five cards in numerical sequence as
　♡3 ♣4 ♡5 ♢6 ♢7)

Flush — any five cards of the same suit

Full house — three of a kind plus a pair

Four of a kind — four cards of the same number

Straight flush — five cards of the same suit in numerical sequence

Royal flush — the ace, king, queen, jack, ten of one suit

Double straight — any ten cards in numerical sequence

Double flush — ten cards of the same suit

Double straight flush — ten cards of the same suit in sequence

BABEL

**For
Six
or
More
Players**

THIS FORM OF BABEL has proved to be a very successful way to start a party. It is an especially exciting game for a group of more than fifteen, and if enough decks of cards are available, there is no limit to the number that can play.

There are, as you will see, quite a few differences between this version of Babel and the standard game for three to five players.

**The
Deal**

THE NUMBER OF DECKS needed for the game is approximately one-third the number of players.

One player acts as scorekeeper and dealer and does not compete in the game. The scorekeeper shuffles all the decks together and deals ten cards to each player. The remainder are placed aside to form the stock pile.

The Play

THE PLAYERS build scoring combinations in their hands by obtaining cards from each other, as in the standard game. In contrast to the standard game, though, players do not sit at a table but are free to move about the room, or from room to room. Players can form groups of two, three, or more to bargain and trade, and they can move from group to group. Those of sufficient voice sometimes announce to the entire party what cards they are looking for, although they often go unheard when everyone else is involved in making deals of his own. By the time a player locates the cards he wants, he usually will have contacted every other player in the game.

Going Out

WHENEVER a player's hand contains *two* Poker combinations of the rank of straight or higher or *one* of the double combinations, he is in a position to go out. (Note that in the standard game of Babel, a straight does *not* help a player to go out, but in this version it does.) A player must keep a hand until he has developed it to the point where he can go out.

Going out does not stop the action for the other players. The player who goes out simply takes his hand over to the scorekeeper and has his score recorded. The scorekeeper places this player's cards on a discard pile and deals him ten new cards from the stock pile. With this new hand the player rejoins the others, who have continued their bargaining and trading.

Whenever the stock pile becomes depleted, the scorekeeper shuffles the cards he has taken in on the discard pile and uses them as a new stock pile.

When a player goes out he must turn in ten cards, even though not all his cards are used for scoring. For instance, if a player has a four of a kind and a straight, he may go out. Only nine of his cards would be used for scoring, but a tenth card would also have to be turned in. Therefore, during the trading, players may not exchange two cards for one card (although this is permitted in the standard game of Babel).

Scoring

SCORING is the same as in the standard game, except that a player may not have a hand scored unless he is in a position to go out. Pairs and threes of a kind are not scored in this game because they are not sufficient to enable you to go out.

Since there is more than one deck, a player is likely to be dealt two or more cards that are identical, that is, cards which have the same number and suit. A player may not use identical cards in the same scoring combination. Thus ♡7 ♠7 ♢7 ♢7 may not be scored as four of a kind since ♢7 appears twice. In like manner ♡A ♡J ♡9 ♡9 ♡2 is not a flush, as there are two ♡9.

Identical cards, however, may be scored twice in a player's hand if they are not both used in the same scoring combination. Thus ♣K-Q-J-10-9 ♣Q-10-5-3-2 may be scored as a straight flush and a flush, for 27 points, even though both the ♣Q and ♣10 appear twice. This hand, however, cannot be scored as a double flush, for 40 points, since a double flush is one combination and the ♣Q and ♣10 would each repeat in it.

Each time the scorekeeper records an individual score, he adds it to that player's previous score. When one player's total score reaches 200, the game is stopped and that player is declared the winner. The other players rank behind him in the order determined by their scores.

Preparations

IF YOU WANT TO TRY this game at a party, here are a few suggestions:

First of all, it shouldn't be necessary to buy extra decks of cards, since some of the guests can be asked to bring their own decks. It's a good idea to shuffle all the cards beforehand and then deal them into packets of ten cards each. This will save time in dealing later. To start the game each player can be handed a packet, and when the players turn in their hands, they can pick up other packets of ten.

A table should be available in one corner of the room for the scorekeeper. Or even better, the scorekeeper can station himself in a room just off the main room. Players will readily travel from room to room, and the scorekeeper can work better in a room away from the main action. If the game is to be an ambitious undertaking of more than fifteen players, it would be advisable to have two scorekeepers.

The scorekeeper should have a sheet of paper with ruled columns on which he can keep each individual's score. It is not necessary to write each person's name on the score sheet before starting the game, for a player's name can be written at the head of a column when he brings in his first scoring hand.

It is a great help in explaining and playing the game if each player can refer to a table that gives the scoring values for the card combinations. Whenever I have given a party at which we played Babel, I provided each player with a slip of paper containing the information below:

Straight .... 5 — any five cards in numerical sequence
Flush .... 7 — any five cards of the same suit
Full house .... 10 — three cards of one rank plus two cards of another rank
Four of a kind .... 15 — four cards of the same rank
Straight flush .... 20 — five cards of the same suit in numerical sequence
Royal flush .... 21 — the ace, king, queen, jack, ten of one suit

Double straight .... 30 — any ten cards in numerical sequence
Double flush .... 40 — ten cards of the same suit
Double straight flush ...... 80 — ten cards of the same suit in sequence

To go out, a player needs two combinations from the first group or one of the double combinations. Duplicate cards may not be used in the same combination.

If you want to avoid writing out such slips, you could include this information on a poster, or it would be possible to explain the scoring verbally.

One advantage to the slips is that they explain the Poker combinations as well as the scoring. Thus those who aren't familiar with Poker hands will be able to play the game. Babel isn't a game like Bridge, where a poor player can spoil the game for the others. It is more like Poker, where the good players (for obvious reasons) will welcome a poor player to their group.

Of course, before the game can be played, you will have to explain it to everyone. The order in which you explain the various points is not too important, but here is a suggestion of how you might go about it: First, distribute the slips that give the information on scoring. Explain that the players will receive ten cards and their object is to score points by getting two Poker hands from the first group or by getting one of the double hands. Explain how the players obtain the cards they want. Be sure to explain that duplicate cards can't be used in the same Poker combination. Then explain how a player can go out, what happens when he goes out, and that the game ends when one player accumulates 200 points.

This game has been tried at many parties, and always with great success. Some players later said that even though they don't like party games, they had a great time with Babel.

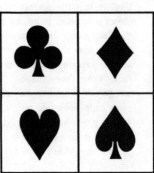

CHAPTER II

LEOPARD

**For
Two
or
Four
Players**

HAVE YOU EVER WANTED TO BE A SABOTEUR?

Do you enjoy the look of shocked disbelief on your opponent's face as his carefully laid plans are upset by your one clever move? Do you chuckle as he gnashes his teeth or kicks the leg of the table?

Of course you do! What healthy, clean-living man — or woman — doesn't?

Then read on!

Learn how you, too, can play a jack on any space of your opponent's square. . . . Learn how this will cancel out the cards under it. . . . Discover how you can evoke consternation by placing a red five between a black four and black six your opponent has played. . . . Watch as he smites his brow!

But hold!

Can you withstand retaliation in kind from a like-minded gamester? Or can you maintain a cheery smile when your opponent, in spite of your best effort, is able to complete his plans and win the hand? If not, you aren't the kind of person who should be playing Leopard.

But if you're a dauntless, right-minded, two-fisted, ten-fingered, courageous card player, then Leopard is your game!

Leopard for two players is described below, and following this are the additional rules that make up a partnership game that four can play.

General Description of Two-Handed Game

THE PLAYERS lay cards on the table to form two squares, one in front of each player. Each square has nine spaces, like a tic-tac-toe grid.

A square is worth two points for every row, column, or diagonal that has three cards of the same suit showing, plus one point for every row, column, or diagonal that shows three cards of the same color but not of the same suit.

Each player tries to build up the value of his square, while keeping down the value of his opponent's. His score for a hand of play is based mainly on what his square is worth at the end of the hand.

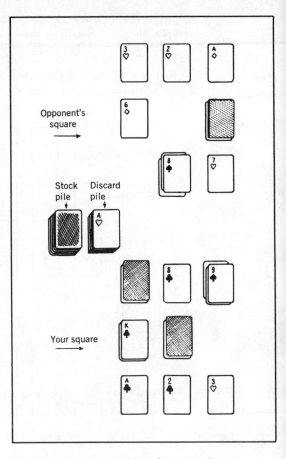

**The
Deal**

TWO STANDARD DECKS (104 cards) are used.

The cards are cut for deal; the player drawing the highest card is dealer (ace is ranked low). If both players draw the same numbered card, they draw again. The deal alternates after each hand.

Eight cards are dealt to each player. The remainder of

23

the pack is placed on one side of the table to form the stock pile. The player opposite the dealer has the first turn.

The Layout

THE FOLLOWING is a diagram of the layout. The nine spaces of each square are numbered as shown:

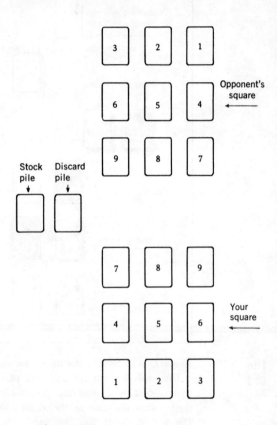

This diagram should be kept in mind, but it need not be

24

marked on the table; for the shape of the layout will become apparent after a few cards have been laid down.

The Play

IN HIS TURN, a player first draws a card from the stock pile and adds it to his hand. He then has a choice either of discarding one card from his hand or of playing one card onto his square or onto his opponent's square. After he plays, the turn passes to his opponent. A card that has been discarded or placed on a square cannot be picked up again by either player.

Various rules govern what cards a player may place on the different spaces of his square or his opponent's square, when he may play a card on top of another card, and what cards are placed face down instead of face up. (Cards that are placed face down on a square do not have their suit or color showing and thus are not counted as part of any scoring line. A space whose top card is face down is considered the same as a blank space and prevents the line it is in from being complete for scoring.)

The rules for the use of each card are given in the following four sections. (These rules are summarized in the chart on page 33.)

The Use of the Cards Ace, Deuce, through Nine

ANY OF THE CARDS ace through nine may be placed only on the space in either square whose number corresponds with the number of the card. That is, an ace may be placed only on the space numbered 1 in your square or on the space numbered 1 in your opponent's square, the deuce may be placed only on the space numbered 2 in either square, etc.

If no cards have as yet been played on your square and you decide to play there, for example, a ◇ 4, then you would place this card in front of you. Wherever you placed it would now be considered the No. 4 space of your square.

If the next card you play on your square is an ♡8, it would be placed in its appropriate space, above and to the right of the ◇4.

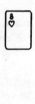

If the next card is a ◇3, it would be placed in its proper space, thus:

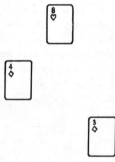

The cards ace through nine are placed face up; they go only in blank spaces or in a space whose top card lies face down.

A player may place any of these cards on his opponent's square as well as his own. If, as in the above example, you had played the ◇4 ♡8 ◇3 on your square, your opponent would assume that you intended to play more red cards on your square. If he had a ♣6 in his hand, he could place it on the No. 6 space of your square.

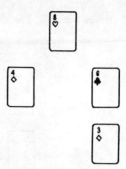

With this ♣6 in place, it is now more difficult for you to put a red card on the No. 6 space. Another six, for instance, could not be placed immediately on top of this ♣6.

The Use of the Ten

A TEN can be placed face up in *any* blank space in your square (or on top of any card in your square that lies face down). *You may not play a ten on your opponent's square.*

A ten is a valuable card to have if it is of the right suit or color. For example, suppose you had this square:

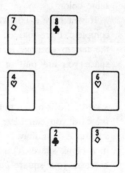

If you put a ♡ 10 in the No. 5 space,

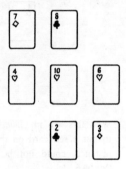

the value of your square would now be 3 points — two points for the horizontal line ♡4 ♡10 ♡6, which are three cards of the same suit, and one point for the diagonal line ◇7 ♡10 ◇3, which are three cards of the same color. The vertical line ♣2 ♡10 ♣8 has no value, since these three cards are neither of the same suit nor of the same color.

If you play a ten when your square is only partially complete, there may be doubt as to what space you mean the ten to occupy. In this case you must declare what space you are putting the ten in.

The Use of the King

A KING, if it is of the right suit or color, is the most powerful card you can have for increasing the value of your square. A king may be put *on top of any card* as well as in a blank space. You may place a king face up in any space in your square *but not in your opponent's.*

For example, the value of the following square in its present condition is 1 point (for the diagonal line of three black cards):

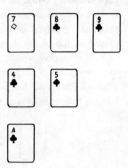

A ♣K could be placed on top of the ◇7,

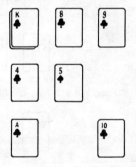

and the value of the square would now be 6 points raw score — two points for the horizontal line ♣K ♣8 ♣9, two points for the vertical line ♣K ♣4 ♣A, one point for the diagonal line ♣K ♠5 ♣10, and one point for the diagonal line ♣A ♠5 ♣9.

As with the ten, if there is any doubt which space you mean a king to occupy, you must declare which space it is on.

The Use of the Jack and Queen

THE JACK AND THE QUEEN can be thought of as portable blank spaces, since they are always played face down. It does not matter what their suits or colors are because they are not counted as part of any scoring line. And any card that can be played on a space that is blank can also be played on top of a jack or queen in that space.

You may play a jack face down on top of *any* card *in your square or in your opponent's square*. This makes it an effective card for sabotage. Suppose your opponent had the following square, which has the value of 4 points:

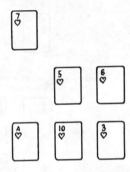

If you put a ♡J on top of the ♡3,

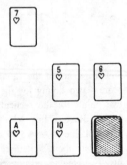

the value of his square would now be zero. Any other

jack could also have been put on the ♡ 3 and the value of the square would still be zero.

You may place a queen face down on top of any card in *your* square *but not in your opponent's.* The following example will show the strategy in playing a queen or jack on your own square.

Suppose you had this square:

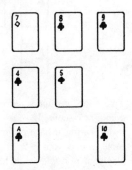

and in your hand you have a ♡ Q and a ♣ 7. When your turn comes, you draw; then you play the ♡ Q face down on the ◇ 7.

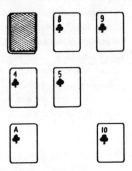

After your opponent has taken his turn, you draw again

from the stock pile and then play the ♣7 in the No. 7 space.

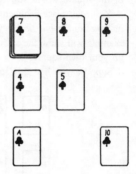

The value of your square has thus been increased to 6 points raw score. If your opponent had had another red seven, he might have put it on your ♡Q before your turn came to play your ♣7. In this case, if you still wanted to play your ♣7, you would have to put down another queen or a jack on the additional red seven.

It is usually the best strategy for a player to try to fill his square with cards of one color. However, he will sometimes find that, after laying a few black cards on his square, his hand contains mainly red cards. If his hand also contains enough queens or jacks, it may be to his advantage to use the queens and jacks to cover up some of the black cards and then to fill his square with the red cards. This process of changing the color of your square is called "changing your spots."

When a jack or queen is discarded, it is placed face up on the discard pile, as are the other cards.

Reference Chart

THE RULES that govern the use of the different cards are summarized in the chart on the next page. You might find this chart helpful as a reference when you try your first hand.

CARD:	MAY BE PLAYED:			
A to 9	Only in space of corresponding number	In either player's square	Only in blank spaces or on top of a card turned face down	Face up only
10	In any numbered space	Only in own square, not in opponent's	Only in blank spaces or on top of a card turned face down	Face up only
J	In any numbered space	In either player's square	On top of anything	Face down only
Q	In any numbered space	Only in own square, not in opponent's	On top of anything	Face down only
K	In any numbered space	Only in own square, not in opponent's	On top of anything (or in blank spaces)	Face up only

Going Out

A PLAYER may go out if the value of his square is 5 points or more and if it is still his turn to play. That is, he can go out only after he has drawn and before making any other play. He cannot go out immediately after having played or discarded a card. Therefore, suppose you have the following square, the value of which is 2:

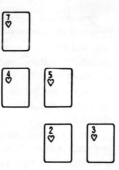

You draw an ♡A from the stock pile and play it. The value of your square is now 6 points raw score. However you cannot go out now; for it is no longer your turn. Your opponent draws and discards. Then you draw; and now you may go out if you wish. If your opponent, instead of discarding, had played a jack on your ♡A, your square would again be worth only 2 points. In this case you could not go out, even after drawing, for your square's value would no longer be 5 points or more.

The player who goes out has one point deducted from his score for the hand. (In this respect Leopard differs from most games, which give a bonus for going out.) This is done to discourage players from going out too fast.

Completing a Hand

WHEN A PLAYER declares that he is out, the hand is complete. If neither player goes out before the stock pile is exhausted, the players continue playing in turn, either discarding a card or playing a card on one of the squares. If still no one has gone out when the last card is played, the hand is complete at this point (and neither player receives the one point deduction for going out).

Scoring

WHEN A HAND IS ENDED, each player's score is figured as follows:

First the raw score value is computed for the player's square in the condition it is in at the end of the hand. As was said before, a square is worth two points for every line that has three cards of the same suit showing plus one point for every line that has showing three cards of the same color but not of the same suit. There are eight lines to a square, three horizontal, three vertical, and two diagonal.

Next a bonus of one point is added for every point the raw score is above 5. In other words, every point above 5 is doubled. The table below gives the value of the score with the bonus for each corresponding value of the raw score:

Raw Score	1	2	3	4	5	6	7	8	9	10	11	12	13	14	15	16
Score with Bonus	1	2	3	4	5	7	9	11	13	15	17	19	21	23	25	27

Finally, one point is subtracted from the score with bonus if the player had gone out this hand.

Thus, what a player scores for a hand of play is the raw score value of his square, plus a bonus of one point for every point the raw score value is above 5, minus one point if the player had gone out.

A game consists of four hands of play. The game scores of the players are totaled after each hand, and the one with the highest after the fourth hand is the winner.

The following are examples of how to compute the raw score value of a square and the score with bonus:

Analysis

♡7	♠8	♠9	 0

♡7 ♠8 ♠9 0
♡4 ♠5 ♣6 0
♡A ♠10 ♣K 0
♡7 ♡4 ♡A 2
♠8 ♠5 ♠10 2
♠9 ♣6 ♣K 1
♡7 ♠5 ♣K 0
♡A ♠5 ♠9 0

total score: 5
(no bonus)

Analysis

◇7	*	♡K	0
◇4	◇5	♡10	1
◇A	*	◇3	0
◇7	◇4	◇A	2
*	◇5	*	0
♡K	♡10	◇3	1
◇7	◇5	◇3	2
◇A	◇5	♡K	1

total raw score: 7
score with bonus: 9
(* *indicates a jack
or queen played
face down*)

Analysis

♣7	blank	◇9	0
♣4	♣5	blank	0
♣10	♣10	♣3	2
♣7	♣4	♣10	2
blank	♣5	♣10	0
◇9	blank	♣3	0
♣7	♣5	♣3	2
♣10	♣5	◇9	0

total raw score: 6
score with bonus: 7

LEOPARD

**for
Four
Players**

IN THE FOUR-PLAYER VERSION, two players are partners against the other two. The partners sit opposite each other. Eight cards are dealt to each player, the player to the left of the dealer goes first, and the turn passes to the left after each play.

There are only two squares to be built upon, one belonging to each side. The cards that make up one side's square are placed in front of either one of the partners.

Any card that a player could play on his square in the two-player game he may play on the square belonging to his side. And any card he could play on his opponent's square he may play on the square belonging to the other side.

The partners may not communicate with each other about the way they think their square should be built. However the players should be able to indicate their preferences by the cards they play. For instance, if the player who goes first places a ♠7 on his side's square, his partner would naturally assume that he wanted them to play black cards and preferably spades. If the first player instead had not played a card on the square but had discarded an ♡A, he might be indicating that he is not sure which color to play but he is a little stronger in black.

During his turn, a player may end the hand by going out. He has the option, however, of first asking his partner if he wants to go out. If the partner says Yes, they then go out; if he says No, they do not go out that turn.

As in the two-player game, the side that goes out has one point deducted from its score. The scoring and the other rules of the two-player game apply here. A game lasts for four hands, giving each player a turn as dealer.

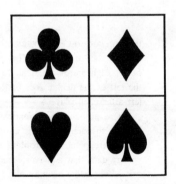

CHAPTER III

AUCTION

**For
Two
to
Seven
Players**

THIS GAME is for people who like auctions. It is also for people who are leery of real auctions because they once wound up owning a moose head, or a ten-dollar piano that cost fifty dollars to transport, or a rug a foot longer than a room. Actually, if it were not for the fact that I like the name Auction better, this game might well have been called White Elephant. In any event, the game is like an auction, but the players bid with cards instead of money.

**General
Description
of
Game**

AUCTION WORKS THIS WAY: Cards that are turned over from the stock pile onto the starter pile are bid for by the players. The one making the highest bid takes the card. What the players offer in exchange, as if it were money, are other cards in their hands.

Each player's object is to get five cards that will make the best Poker hand in a showdown at the end of the bidding. (Those who are not familiar with Poker hands will find them explained on page 46.)

Preliminary

WHEN TWO OR THREE PLAY, use one deck of cards with two jokers (54 cards in all). When four or more play, use two decks plus four jokers (108 cards).

All the cards, including the jokers, are shuffled together, and ten cards are dealt to each player. The remainder of the deck is placed face down to form the stock pile. The top card of this pile is turned over and placed next to the stock pile. This card is the first card of the starter pile, and the first card to be bid on.

**Bidding
a
Single
Card**

THE PLAYERS do not take turns in the bidding. Any time a player wants the top card, he simply calls out a bid. If another player also wants that top card, or wants to keep the first player from getting it, that player then calls out a higher bid. A player may drop out or rejoin the bidding whenever he wishes.

Single cards are ranked this way: joker highest, followed by ace, king, on down to deuce. Cards of the same number are ranked spade, heart, diamond, club. Suits thus affect the ranking of single cards in this game. But when a pair or higher combination is involved, the suits are all considered equal and do not affect the rank of these combinations.

When a player bids a single card, he calls out the number of that card. He need not name its suit at first. However, if a second player wishes to bid a card of the same number, he must call out the suit as well as the number. If the first player then wishes to rebid his card, he must name its suit as well.

When there are two decks being used in the game, there is the possibility that two players will bid cards of identical number and suit. In this case the player who first called out that *number* is considered to have made the higher bid.

Here is an example of bidding:

There are four players, and the top card of the starter pile is a jack of diamonds.

> Smith: "I bid a two."
>
> Jones: "Four."
>
> Robinson: "Four of hearts." Jones's four was only a diamond; so he does not rebid it.
>
> Jones: "Seven."
>
> Smith: "Seven of diamonds."
>
> Jones: "Seven of spades."
>
> Smith: "Eight."
>
> Robinson: "Nine."
>
> Jones: "Nine of hearts."
>
> Robinson: "My nine was also hearts." Robinson thus is considered to have made the highest bid at this point because he bid a nine first.
>
> Smith: "Jack."
>
> Brown: "Joker."
>
> Brown, who had not previously made a bid, decided to enter the bidding at this point and named the highest single card. If no player bids a pair or a higher combination, Brown is considered to have won the bidding.

Of course, if a player has made a bid and no one bids higher, he may not back down. If a player is unable to produce what he bid, the other players may, if they wish, assess a 15-point penalty against him (although most players excuse honest mistakes).

When a player wins the bid with a single card, he does the following, in the order indicated:

1. He removes the top card from the starter pile.
2. He places the card he bid onto the top of the starter pile.
3. He turns over the top card of the stock pile and places it on top of the starter pile.
4. He puts the card he won into his hand.

The cards on the starter pile should not be placed directly on top of each other but should be fanned out slightly so that each one is visible.

When a new card is turned over from the stock pile, the players may begin bidding on it. If no one wants to bid on a card, another is turned over from the stock pile and placed on top of it.

Bidding
a
Pair
or
Higher
Combination

BESIDES being able to bid a single card, a player may bid a pair or a higher Poker combination at any time. Thus the bidding in a game might sound like this:

Robinson: "I bid a seven."
Smith: "King."
Jones: "Pair of sixes."
Robinson: "Two jokers."
Smith: "Three twos."
Jones: "A straight."
Robinson: "A flush."
Jones: "A flush with queen high."
Robinson: "My flush has ace high."
Jones: "Full house."

Whenever a player bids a pair, three of a kind, or four of a kind, he must name the rank of the cards. However, when bidding a straight, flush, full house, or straight flush, he need only give the name of the combination. Only if two players name the same combination must they decide whose cards rank higher. If the cards in the two combinations rank exactly equal, the player who first bid the combination is considered higher.

Two cards identical in suit and number cannot be used in one combination. Thus ♡8 ♡8 cannot be bid as a pair of eights nor ◇Q ◇10 ◇7 ◇7 ◇2 as a flush. Identical cards also may not be used in the showdown at the end of a hand.

Jokers are not wild cards in this game. They cannot be used in combination with other cards or in the showdown hand at the end. Players may bid jokers either singly or with other jokers in pairs or as three or four of a kind, beating any other pair, three, or four of a kind. (Jokers may not be used as part of a full house.)

When a player wins the bidding with a combination, he obtains a number of cards from the top of the *starter* pile equal to the number of cards he bid. Thus if a player wins the bidding with a pair, he obtains the top card of the pile as well as the card directly under it. If he bid a three of a kind, he takes the top three cards of the pile. If he bid a four of a kind, he takes the top four cards; and if he had bid a straight, a flush, a full house, or a straight flush, he would take the top five cards of the pile.

The Poker hand of two pairs, because it is comparatively easy to get, is not used for bidding in this game and therefore could not be used to take four cards from the starter pile.

The player who wins the bidding with a combination follows the same general procedure as when a single card is the top bid. Suppose the top bid is this straight: ♡4, ♡5 ♠6 ◇7 ♠8. The player who made that bid:

1. Removes the top five cards from the starter pile.
2. Next he places his straight on top the starter pile. The cards in the straight should overlap, leaving each card visible, *but the player may arrange them in any order he wishes.* For instance, he might place the cards so that the ♠6 is on top, the ♡4 directly under it, next the ♡5, then the ♠8, and then the

◇ 7. But once they are placed on the pile, the order of the cards *may not be changed.*

3. He turns over the top card of the stock pile and places it on top the starter pile.

4. Then he puts the five cards he won into his hand.

Early in a hand, if a player bids a combination that has more cards than there are in the starter pile, here's what happens:

1. The player removes the entire starter pile.

2. He places the combination he bid down to start a new starter pile.

3. He turns over the top card from the stock pile and places it on top of the cards he bid.

4. He puts the card or cards he won into his hand.

5. He draws from the top of the stock pile enough additional cards to again bring the amount of cards in his hand to ten. He does not show the cards he draws to the other players.

At the start of a hand, it may be wise to bid more cards than there are in the starter pile, just to get different cards from the stock. For instance, suppose you are dealt this hand: ♠K ♠J ♠J ♣J ◇8 ♠7 ♣6 ♡5 ◇4 ♠2. The straight, 8 through 4, is not very valuable because it may be difficult to develop it into anything better. Therefore, at the start of the play, you could offer this straight as a bid. If you won the auction, you would obtain one card from the starter pile plus four unknown cards from the stock pile. The chances are you would then have a hand of greater potential than the one you were dealt.

Tactics ONE OF THE MAIN ADVANTAGES of bidding a pair or higher is that it gives you the opportunity to pick up cards that other players have already put on the starter pile. Since a new card from the stock pile is always turned over to cover the cards previously bid, it is impossible to get one of these previous cards if you bid only a single card. So even though you may not want the top card of the starter pile, it may be worth bidding a pair and taking it just to get the card underneath.

In fact, a player should always keep in mind the top *five* cards of the starter pile. For if he can use any or all of these cards to make better combinations with the cards in his hand, he should consider bidding to get them. Sometimes very intricate gambits can be carried out. For instance, there are occasions when it is important for you to win a bid, but to do so you would have to use cards vital to your hand. Often you can bid these vital cards and later retrieve them by bidding other cards (sometimes even by bidding some of the cards you won when you bid the vital cards).

There's a surprising amount of strategy in Auction that is not at first apparent, and you should discover more each time you play.

Ending a Hand of Play

THERE ARE three ways a hand is ended. One is when a joker is turned over from the stock pile onto the starter pile. The players, of course, never know when this might happen, but when it does the play stops and the winner of the hand is decided at that point. The hand does not end, of course, when players bid jokers from their hand and place them on the starter pile.

A hand also ends when the stock pile is depleted. After the last card is turned over, players may still bid on that card. But once someone has won the bid and taken that card, the hand is over.

A third way a hand ends is when a player goes out. Players may not go out before eight cards have accumulated on the starter pile. But after there are eight or more cards on the pile, a player may go out any time he wishes, even in the midst of bidding. If the one who goes out is subsequently found to be the winner of the hand, he is given a 10-point bonus in addition to the other points he scores. If he does not win the hand or only ties for winner, 25 points are deducted from his score. If the player receiving this penalty previously had less than 25 points in his total score, his score becomes a minus number.

Scoring

WHEN A HAND IS ENDED, each player picks out five of his cards. He cannot include any identical cards or jokers among the five. *The player whose five cards make the best Poker hand is the winner of that hand of play.* If two or more players tie, they divide the winning score.

The winner's score is determined by the cards left in the starter pile at the end of the hand. For each ace in this pile he scores 10 points; for each king, queen, jack, or joker, 5 points; and for each card deuce through ten, one point.

The winner's score as well as any bonus or penalty given a player who goes out is added to the previous game scores. The game is won by the first player to make 150 points.

The Rank of the Hands

THE FINAL SHOWDOWN hand — that is, the hand a player chooses to represent him — contains five cards with no identical cards or jokers. The highest hand is the one that contains the highest Poker combination. These combinations rank as follows, from highest to lowest:

Straight flush — five cards of the same suit in numerical sequence
Four of a kind — four cards of the same rank
Full house — three of a kind plus a pair
Flush — any five cards of the same suit
Straight — any five cards in numerical sequence
Three of a kind — three cards of the same rank
Two pair — two cards of one rank plus two cards of another rank
(This hand may be used in the showdown, although it is not used in bidding.)
Pair — two cards of the same rank

If two hands contain the same combination, the higher of the two is determined this way: First, only the cards that make up the combination are considered. For instance, the three-of-a-kind hand has three cards that make up the combination and two cards left over that fill out the hand. The hand that contains the highest card in the combination is considered the higher hand. If both hands have the same high card, then the next highest card in each are compared, and if these are the same, the next highest are compared, and so on. An ace is always considered high except when it is part of the straight or straight flush A-2-3-4-5, which is considered the lowest straight or straight flush. The highest straight flush, A-K-Q-J-10 of one suit, is also called a royal flush. A straight or straight flush may not "turn the corner," such as Q-K-A-2-3.

The one exception is the full house: the higher full house is the one whose three of a kind ranks higher. If both threes of a kind are of the same rank, then the rank of the pairs is compared.

If the cards that make up the combination in each hand are all of the same rank, then the other cards, if any, that fill out the five-card hand are considered. The hand that contains the highest of these is higher; if both have this same high card, then the next highest cards are compared, and so on.

If two hands are equal in all respects, they tie. No one suit ranks above another in the showdown hand.

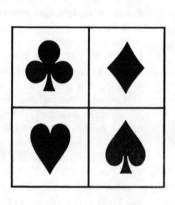

CHAPTER IV

VARIETY

**For
Four
Players**

TWO OF THE MOST COMMON PROBLEMS in an evening of cards often turn out to be bad hands and dull partners. That is why I have developed a game in which there is no such thing as a bad hand (if you play it right) and your partner may change with every hand.

Variety, appropriately enough, is not a single game but eight different ones, each of which involves a somewhat different form of trick-taking. Each time the cards are dealt, you start anew, knowing neither which game you will be playing or who your partner will be. Much of Variety's strategy involves evaluating your cards in order to pick the right game and the right partner.

This game and the one that follows, Metamorphosis, are variants on traditional trick-taking games such as Hearts and Whist. If you are not familiar with trick-taking in general, read the next section. If you are, then skip to the instructions starting on page 50.

Trick-Taking

TO START A TRICK, the person who plays first picks any card from his hand and lays it face up in the center of the table. The player on the left plays a card next; after each player has laid down one card, the trick is complete.

A player must "follow suit" if he can, that is he must play a card of the same suit as the first card played. If he has no cards of the suit that was led, he may then play any card he wishes.

Whoever plays the highest card of the suit led wins the trick. However, if one suit is designated as trump and if any cards of the trump suit have been played, then the highest trump wins the trick.

A player is not forced to trump. For example, suppose hearts are trump and the first card led is a spade. You have no spades in your hand, but you do have hearts. You have the choice of playing a heart and possibly winning the trick or, if it is advantageous to you, of playing a diamond or club and losing the trick.

The player who wins a trick leads the first card to the next trick.

In winning a trick, a player wins the cards in the trick. Partners combine the tricks each of them wins. And, depending on the game, scoring is determined by the number of tricks won or by certain of the cards taken in the tricks.

The Deal

VARIETY uses a standard deck of fifty-two cards. The cards are cut for deal, and the player drawing the highest card is dealer. Ace ranks high. If two or more players draw the same high card, there is another drawing for those who tie. The deal passes to the left after each hand.

The entire deck is dealt out to the four players.

Determining the Game

THE CHART ON THE NEXT PAGE lists the eight games it is possible to choose to play. This chart isn't as complicated as it first appears. The column on the left lists the cards that are most valuable for winning each game. When a player is trying to decide which game his hand is best suited for, he should consult this left-hand column. For instance, if his hand is strong in spades, he would want to play games No. 5, 3, or perhaps 1. If he has a hand that contains mainly low cards, he would want to play No. 6, 7, or 8.

This chart can be passed around to each player when he is deciding which game he wants to play. Or, even better, you might make copies of it.

GAME NUMBER	MOST VALUABLE CARDS FOR WINNING	RULES OF THE GAME
1.	High cards	No trump — the side taking the longest suit scores 12 points (if tie, no score)
2.	Clubs	Clubs trump — every trick counts plus 2
3.	Hearts-Spades	Hearts trump — every spade taken counts plus 2
4.	Diamonds-Hearts	Diamonds trump — red cards count plus 1, black cards count minus 1
5.	Spades-Clubs	Spades trump — the black 10's and jacks each count plus 5, the red 10's and jacks each count minus 5
6.	Clubs (low cards)	Clubs trump — lowest card takes trick — every red card counts plus 1
7.	Hearts-Diamonds (low cards)	Spades trump — every club counts minus 2
8.	Low cards	No trump — every trick counts minus 2

The column on the right gives the rules for each particular game, stating whether any suit is trump and how the hand is scored. Game No. 6 is the only exception to normal trick-taking play: in that game the lowest card, or the lowest trump, takes the trick.

After the hands are dealt, the game to be played and

51

the partners are determined as follows: Starting to the left of the dealer, each player in turn proposes a game he would like to play. A player must name a game each time it is his turn, even if he feels there is no game he could do well in. As soon as a second player names a game that has already been named, that is the one to be played, and the two who named it are partners against the other two.

Here is an example of the way the process works: Smith, the player to the left of the dealer, names game No. 3. If Jones, the next player, also chooses No. 3, that game must then be played, even though the other two players have not had a chance to name their choices. Smith and Jones would in this case be partners against the other two. Suppose, however, that Jones does not want to play No. 3, and instead names game No. 1. The choice now goes to the next player, Robinson. Robinson can either play game No. 3 with Smith as his partner, game No. 1 with Jones as his partner, or he can propose another game. Say he names game No. 2 instead. It is now the turn of the dealer, Brown, to name a game. Brown does not like any of the three named so far, so he proposes No. 8.

Since no game has been decided on yet, the turn goes back to Smith, who now must make a second proposal. He may not re-make his original proposal. This time he names game No. 5. Smith has now proposed both No. 3 and No. 5. Next it is Jones's turn to make a second proposal. He names game No. 3, Smith's original proposal. Game No. 3 is therefore the game to be played, and Smith and Jones are partners against Robinson and Brown.

Even though a game has been decided on for one hand of play, it can be proposed again during later hands.

The Play

THE TWO PLAYERS who named the game are referred to as the "declarers," and the other two are the "defenders."

The players do not change their seats, because it is not necessary for partners to sit opposite each other.

The lead is made by the first defender to the left of the declarer who first proposed the game being played. The turn to play passes to the left, and the player who wins one trick leads to the next.

If the defenders are able to score more than the declarers, they receive a 10-point bonus in addition to their regular score.

Scoring

THE SCORE *each* player receives for a hand of play is the total score *his side* receives. Since the partnerships are always shifting, the game scores for each player are kept separately. A player's game score may be either a plus or a minus number.

Here is an example of scoring: Smith and Brown are the declarers playing game No. 4 against Jones and Robinson. Smith and Brown take in three red cards and nine black cards. The score for their side is therefore minus 6. Jones and Robinson take in twenty-three red cards and seventeen black. Their score is therefore plus 6, and since they were the defenders and scored more than the declarers, they receive a 10-point bonus, which makes their score 16. Thus 16 points are added to Jones's game score, 16 points are added to Robinson's score, 6 points are subtracted from Smith's score, and 6 points are subtracted from Brown's game score.

A game of Variety consists of eight hands of play, or, if the players desire a shorter game, they may agree to only four hands. The player with the highest score at the end is the winner.

Advertising

THERE IS NO PROHIBITION against a player giving information about his hand before a game is decided on. In fact, if a player has an especially good hand for a particular game, it may be necessary for him to advertise its value in order to obtain a partner. For instance, if a player had all the high clubs, he would propose playing game No. 2. But since no one else would have any good clubs, it would be difficult to find a second person to name this game. Therefore, he might say to the player on his left, "Pick number 2. I've got most of the clubs, and with me as your partner, you'll clean up!"

If a player exaggerates the value of his hand, he may gain a partner but lose the game and give the defenders the 10-point bonus. Also, a player might find he is advertising to the wrong person. For example, his touting the strength of his hand in spades might persuade someone to pick a game where spades are a liability. Furthermore, any information a player gives to his future partner will also be used by his future opponents.

Once a game has been chosen, players are not permitted to give additional information to each other.

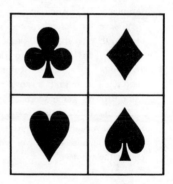

CHAPTER V

METAMORPHOSIS

**For
Two
or
Three
Players**

THIS GAME is called Metamorphosis because, like the caterpillar that becomes a butterfly, it changes as you play it. What is more, unlike the caterpillar and the butterfly, Metamorphosis changes three times, not just once. So, if you are the sort of person whose interest flags when he plays the same game all evening, try Metamorphosis; all you have to do is wait a few minutes and you'll be playing another game.

General Description

A SET IN METAMORPHOSIS consists of four hands of play, each of which involves a different type of trick-taking. The cards a player wins in one hand are used by him to play the next hand.

The play in each of these four hands is simple. But multiple strategies are open to a player who considers the game as a whole. For example, while playing Hand 1, he will be concerned, of course, with scoring high on that hand. But, at the same time, he will be building up good cards with which to play Hand 2. And he may even be tempering these strategies with considerations of what sort of cards he can expect in Hand 3 or 4.

The Deal

TWO DECKS OF CARDS are needed to play Metamorphosis. A standard deck of fifty-two cards is used. In addition, each player takes the ace, 2, 3, and 4 of any one suit out of the second deck. The remaining cards of the second deck are not used in the game.

The four cards taken by each player are his "indicator" cards; their purpose is explained later. These cards are kept separate from the hand the player is dealt.

The deck of fifty-two cards is cut for deal, and the player drawing the highest card is dealer (ace is high). If more than one person draws the same high card, there is another drawing for those who tie.

Each player is dealt twelve cards, and the rest of the deck is placed face down to form the stock pile.

Using the Indicator Cards

THE TABLE BELOW lists the way each of the four hands is played. Readers who aren't familiar with this sort of trick-taking will find it described on page 50.

Hand 1. No trump — every club taken counts minus 4.
Hand 2. Diamonds trump — every heart counts plus 3.
Hand 3. No trump — every card taken counts minus 1.
Hand 4. No trump — every spade counts plus 4.

After a player has examined his cards, he chooses the one

hand of the four he thinks he has a good chance of winning. He then picks from his indicator cards the one that corresponds to the hand number he chose and places it face down in front of him. For instance, if he thinks he can win Hand 1, he places the ace in front of him, or if he thinks he can win Hand 2, he puts down the deuce.

After every person has placed a card on the table, the cards are turned face up to reveal the choices. The indicator cards are then put aside, but with the card of each player's choice still visible.

Later, a bonus of ten points is given to anyone who actually wins in the hand he indicated. If a player only ties for winner in his chosen hand, he does not receive the ten-point bonus.

Hand 1

THE FIRST LEAD is made by the player to the left of the dealer. As the table shows, this hand is played no-trump, and four points are scored *against* a player for every club he takes in. After the scores are recorded, each player picks up *every* card he took in and uses them for Hand 2.

Hand 2

AT THIS POINT one player may have more cards than another. Before the hand can be played, everyone must have twelve cards again.

If a player has less than twelve, he draws from the stock until he has twelve. The cards drawn are not shown to the other players.

If a player has more than twelve, he discards his excess. Deciding what cards to discard is an important part of the strategy. The discards must not be seen by the other players; they are placed on a separate pile.

The player who led first in Hand 1 leads first in Hand 2. Diamonds are trump, and a player scores three points for every heart he takes in. The cards a player wins are used to play Hand 3.

Hand 3

IF THE AMOUNT OF CARDS in each hand is not twelve at the start of this hand, the hands must be equalized again. But the method of equalization differs from that used in Hand 2. The method used in this hand resembles the game of Old Maid. A player who has more than twelve cards holds his hand up with the backs of the cards facing his opponents. An opponent with less than twelve then picks enough cards so that each will again have twelve. There is of course no strategy in this process, as a player does not know what he is picking.

The first lead is made by the player to the left of the one who led first in Hands 1 and 2. There is no trump, and *every* card a player takes scores one point *against* him. The cards taken in this hand are used to play Hand 4.

Hand 4

THE METHOD OF EQUALIZING the amounts of cards before Hand 4 is the same as that used before Hand 2. Everyone either draws or discards until the total amount of cards each has is twelve.

If the stock pile becomes depleted, the cards of the discard pile are shuffled and used as a new stock. This is done before any new discards are added; that is, a player who needs to draw cards does so before another player makes any discards. (If, in the three-player game, players need to draw more cards than are in both piles, they first take as many as they can and then take more after the other player has discarded.)

The first lead is made by the same player who led first in Hand 3. The play is no-trump, and every spade taken scores four points.

Sets

THESE FOUR HANDS of play make up a set. After Hand 4 is finished, all fifty-two cards are shuffled together and dealt for the next set. The dealer is the player to the left of the dealer of the previous set.

Four sets (sixteen hands of play) make a game when two play. Three sets (twelve hands of play) constitute a game when three play. Whoever ends up with the highest score wins.

The following is an example of the scoring of one set during a three-player game:

	Smith	Jones	Robinson
Hand 1	− 32	0*	0
Hand 2	+15*	+3	+ 9
Hand 3	− 24	−9	− 3*
Hand 4	+44	+4	0
Bonus	+10		+10
Total	13	− 2	16

The asterisks here indicate the hand each player chose by his indicator card. Although Smith did much better in Hand 4 than in Hand 2, he received the bonus for picking Hand 2, because he did beat both his opponents in that hand. Jones picked Hand 1 and got a perfect score in that hand, because he avoided taking in any clubs. But he did not receive a bonus, since Robinson tied his score. Robinson picked Hand 3 and received a bonus for getting the best score in that hand.

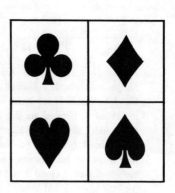

SWITCH

For
Two
or
Four
Players

PARTNERSHIP GAMES are often very annoying, sometimes even unhealthy. For instance, suppose you're stuck with a bad partner who also happens to be your wife. She makes a particularly stupid play. Your first impulse is to say something to her; but, since most partnership games forbid communication, you must suppress the impulse. Bawling out your wife might betray information about your hand. Instead you reflect darkly on her mistake, magnifying it out of proportion. Only when the game is over do you confront her with The Error. She then calmly explains that hers was the only correct play and your own strategy was faulty. Since you're forced to admit the truth of her assertion, this reversal further undermines your mental health.

Fortunately there's no need to undergo expensive psychotherapy in order to continue playing partnership games. Switch offers symptomatic relief and attacks the cause of partnership dissent.

Specifically, in Switch all the cards are played face up, so that each player has all the information he wants about his partner's and opponents' possible plays. There is no rule against communication among players; instead, communication is encouraged. Players who happen to be in partnership will be able to discuss their plans and agree on what moves each should make. The only restriction on these discussions is that they may not be in private; thus the opponents will be able to hear any plans partners choose to discuss. This leads to the interesting situation in which opposing sides not only have total information about each other's hands but also know pretty much what the others are thinking. Sometimes towards the end of a hand both sides get together and discuss all possible sequences of moves each could make, and in this way a perfect strategy for one side may be discovered.

Switch is not, strictly speaking, a partnership game but rather is one of shifting alliances. Each player is scored individually and each works only for himself in terms of the complete game. But during each hand of play, an alliance of two players is formed against the other two; and this alliance lasts through that hand only.

This is the part of Switch that allows you to escape bad partners. In every new hand you have a chance to choose a different partner. And your choice does not even have to be made at the beginning of the hand! Instead you can wait to see how the others are doing and you might then be able to join forces with the strongest player. If this seems like too ideal a situation, I should explain that, if someone else makes a choice before you, your partner for the hand is then determined. Also, the player who does the choosing may score only a reduced number of points if his side wins the hand. The question of whether or not to choose a partner or whom to choose is an important part of the strategy.

The game for four players is described below and following it is a version for two players.

Equipment

A STANDARD DECK of 52 cards is used.

Also, four markers are to be used as pieces representing the four players. Any four objects will work as long as each is distinct from the others. Most often I use the king, queen, knight, and rook from a Chess set.

The Deal

THE CARDS ARE CUT for deal; the player drawing the lowest card is dealer (ace is high). If there is a tie for low, there is another drawing for those who tie. The deal passes to the left after each hand.

The deck is shuffled, and the dealer deals out six rows of cards, each row containing six cards face up. The remainder of the deck is placed aside and is not used during the hand.

The 36 cards dealt on the table should form a square of straight rows and columns, as in the illustration on the next page. Each player places his piece on the card at the left end of the row (or column) nearest him, as in the illustration.

**Typical
Layout
at
the
Start
of
a
Hand**

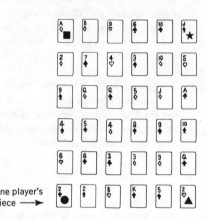

One player's
piece ——→

**General
Description
of
Game**

THE PLAYERS move their pieces over this array of cards in
a fashion similar to that of board games. Therefore, the
array should be thought of as a playing board, with each
of the 36 cards representing a space. Later, even though
cards are removed from the array, this imaginary board
should still be thought of as having 36 spaces. Usually
enough cards will remain to indicate where the rows and
columns are.

Whenever your piece lands on a card, you remove that
card from the array and add it to your hand. At the start
of each new hand of play, your object is to acquire cards
from which you can select the best five-card Poker hand.
Later, however, your object may become that of seeing
that your partner acquires the best hand.

Readers who are not familiar with Poker hands will
find them described on page 72.

**Typical
Layout
During
the
Middle
of
a
Hand**

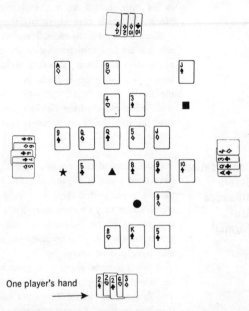

One player's hand ➡️

Moves

THE FIRST MOVE is made by the player to the left of the dealer, and after him the turn passes to the left.

In his turn a player moves his piece any number of spaces along a row or column (but never diagonally), provided that this move is not made onto or over a space occupied by another player's piece.

A player may make his move onto or over blank spaces as well as spaces occupied by cards.

If a player ends his turn on a card, he removes that card and places it face up in front of him. Cards thus acquired become part of the player's hand but must remain visible.

If a player ends his turn on a blank space, he receives no card during that turn.

A player must move one or more spaces each time it

is his turn, unless he is completely blocked by other pieces, in which case he simply misses a turn.

Since a player must move his piece each turn, he may not use his first turn to acquire the card his piece is on at the start of a hand (although he may come back for it later). An exception is made in the rare instance when the dealer finds he cannot move during his first turn, since other players have blocked him completely. In this case the card he is on becomes part of his hand.

Conversation Before Alliances Are Formed

ALLIANCES are usually not formed until after several moves have been made in a hand of play. Although this means there are no partnerships discussing their strategy, the conversation may be even more lively at this point. What is said, of course, depends on the personality of the group, but the following are some suggestions of comments that have proved useful:

If one player is acquiring a good hand, point out that he should be stopped from getting other valuable cards. This is especially useful if you are unable or unwilling to stop him yourself. (A player may be blocked temporarily from getting a card if another player moves his piece onto a space between that player's piece and the card. A player may be stopped permanently from getting a card if another player picks up that card instead.)

If another player points out that you yourself are acquiring a good hand, cry poverty. Say, "Me! I'll only have a lousy straight. Him! He's the one you should worry about."

An alternative strategy is to call attention to the strength of your position in hopes of finding someone who will want you as a partner.

If you do make a move that will block a strong player, state (humbly) what a noble sacrifice you are making for the other two players in wasting your own turn to block the strong player. This is even more effective if you only appear to be blocking the strong player but are actually moving into a position where you can acquire much better cards for yourself.

(In case you consider such deceptions and admonitions to be undignified in a game of skill, it should be noted that game theory concerns itself with conflicts quite similar to these and with the problems involved in shifting alliances.)

Alliances

A PLAYER may form an alliance during his turn and before he moves his piece for that turn. He forms the alliance simply by stating that he is entering a partnership with a certain other player. He is then allied with that player against the other two players for the duration of that hand. The partner chosen cannot refuse the offer of partnership.

For example, suppose the four players are Smith, Jones, Robinson, and Brown. Smith has given up hope of obtaining the best hand, but he thinks Jones is in a good position to win, especially if he gives Jones some help. It is Smith's turn to move; so he says something to this effect: "I hereby form a partnership with Jones." Thus Smith and Jones are allied against Robinson and Brown. As indicated, Jones has no say-so as to whether he wants Smith for a partner, nor can Robinson and Brown avoid being allied at this point. During each hand there is only one opportunity for a choice to be made, because when one player chooses a partner, that defines the opposing sides for the rest of the hand.

The existence of partnerships does not change the rules of play. The partners do not combine their hands, but each continues to acquire cards for himself. The only way a player may help his partner is by using his piece to block opponents' pieces or by picking up cards that might be valuable to the opponents.

The only change that results from the formation of

partnerships is in the scoring at the end of the hand. Each player scores differently depending on whether the winner of the hand is the one who chose a partner, whether he is the partner chosen, or whether he is one of their opponents.

HERE ARE THE RULES FOR SCORING:

The player who chose *a partner will score 3 points only if his partner wins the hand. If he himself wins, no one scores anything.*

The player who was chosen *will score 7 points only if he himself wins.*

If the winner is either one of the players opposing *the one who chose and the one chosen, this winner will score 6 points and his partner will score 4.*

As you can see, the player who does the choosing gives himself a handicap. He can score only if his partner wins, and then he scores only 3 points while his partner scores 7. This player, therefore, will work only for his partner.

The players opposing the one who chose are in a partnership of a different nature. They can score if either one of them wins; however, the winner scores 6 points and his partner 4. This 2-point difference can cause some conflict of interest. Either of these players would be happy to see his partner win, but he may not always help his partner, since he can score more by winning himself. Their alliance is therefore not as tightly knit as the one between the other two players.

These rules will be further clarified by the example of scoring given on page 70.

If no player were to choose a partner during a hand, the winner would score 10 points.

Ending a Hand

THEORETICALLY the hand ends when all the cards in the array have been picked up or when blocking by one side makes it impossible to acquire any more cards. In practice, though, the players can end the hand when they see that one of them is in an unbeatable position.

The winning player is the one who has acquired five cards that make the best poker hand. Even if the winning player doesn't want to win (as is sometimes the case if he is the one who chose his partner), his best selection of five cards is still used instead of any other of his cards. If there is a tie for best hand, there is no score.

After each player's score is recorded, all 52 cards are shuffled together, and a new array of cards is then dealt.

Scoring 16 or More Points

TO WIN THE GAME a player needs 20 points. However, when a player's total score nears 20, the others often gang up on him to keep him from winning. Even his partner might want to play against him. To prevent a temporary stalemate from occuring at this point, any player who has a total score of 16 or more points is given a special power. *He makes the moves of his partner's piece as well as his own.* This power may be used to help or hinder the partner. A player with 16 or more points may try to achieve a win for his partner, or he may make sure his partner doesn't win.

This may seem like a drastic weapon to give a player who is already ahead, but it is the only means a leading player will have for breaking the coalition that is sure to be formed against him by the other three players.

If two players in partnership both have scores of 16 or more points, then this power does not apply, even if one of the players has a higher score than the other. Neither player will be able to move the piece of the other.

Winning the Game

WHEN A PLAYER'S total score reaches 20 points, he wins the game. However, if two partners both reach 20 in the same hand, the one who then has the highest score wins. (This may serve as a restraint on your choice of partner

69

towards the end of a game.) If there is a tie for highest at this point, additional hands are played until one player (not necessarily one of those tying originally) gets the highest score.

The following is an example of the scoring in one game.

HOW HAND WAS PLAYED	SMITH	JONES	ROBINSON	BROWN
Smith formed partnership with Jones. Jones won.	3	7	0	0
Jones formed partnership with Brown. Robinson won.	4	0	6	0
Total scores	7	7	6	0
Smith formed partnership with Brown. Smith won.	0	0	0	0
Total scores	7	7	6	0
Robinson formed partnership with Smith. Jones won.	0	6	0	4
Total scores	7	13	6	4
Robinson formed partnership with Smith. Smith won.	7	0	3	0
Total scores	14	13	9	4
Brown formed partnership with Smith. Robinson won.	0	4	6	0
Total scores	14	17	15	4
Jones formed partnership with Brown. Since Jones's total score was 17 points, he made all of Brown's moves after Brown became his partner. He played so that Brown won the hand. Jones thereby won the game.	0	3	0	7
Total scores	14	20	15	11

SWITCH

**for
Two
Players**

THE TWO-PLAYER GAME follows the same rules as that for four except that only 25 cards, five rows of five each, are dealt onto the table. The players sit opposite each other, and each places his piece on the card at the left end of the row nearest him. The winner of a hand scores 10 points, and 40 points wins the game.

There are, of course, no partnerships in this version, and thus it doesn't have the same interest as the four-player game, but there are still opportunities for strategy. In fact, a little analysis of the game shows that for every array of cards dealt there must exist a perfect winning strategy for one of the players. An interesting fact is that this strategy is different for each new array dealt. The complete strategy of a hand, though, is usually much too complex to be discovered at the start of the hand.

Poker Hands

THE FOLLOWING IS the rank of the Poker hands from highest to lowest:

Straight flush—five cards of the same suit in numerical sequence
Four of a kind—four cards of the same rank
Full house—three of a kind plus a pair
Flush—any five cards of the same suit
Straight—any five cards in numerical sequence
Three of a kind—three cards of the same rank
Two pair—two cards of one rank plus two cards of another rank
Pair—two cards of the same rank

THE HIGHER of two *straights* or two *straight flushes* is the one which has the highest card. Ace is always high except in the sequence A-2-3-4-5. The higher of two *fours of a kind,* two *threes of a kind,* or two *pairs* is determined by the rank of the cards making up the combination. The higher of two *full houses* is the one that contains the higher ranking *three of a kind.* The higher of two *flushes* is determined by the rank of the highest card in each. If both high cards are the same, the next highest are compared, and so on. Two hands that are equal in all respects tie. No one suit ranks above another.

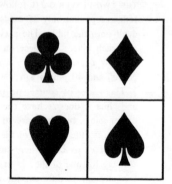

CHAPTER VII

ELEUSIS

For
Three
or
More
Players

NO MATTER how many card games you know and have played, I think it is a safe bet that you have never played one like Eleusis (pronounced El-lew′sis). That's because Eleusis is virtually in a class by itself and works in a manner quite different from almost all other games.

Normally, a game has a set of rules that every player knows in advance. The big difference in Eleusis is that you start a hand without knowing the key rule that governs the play of that hand. Figuring out this secret rule will help you make the right plays and will probably enable you to win. But the rule changes with every hand. This can create interesting, not to say perplexing, situations.

Eleusis was first introduced in the June 1959 issue of *Scientific American* in the "Mathematical Games" department. Since then it has created a surprising amount of interest in the scientific world, not only as an enjoyable pastime but also in a wide variety of other applications.

For instance, a research psychologist at one of the large defense systems corporations is using Eleusis as an experimental medium with which to study inductive reasoning in humans. He wrote me that one of the reasons for his interest in Eleusis is that it is "analogous to certain types of military problems that we are vitally concerned with." One of the things he is investigating is the influence of various machine and display techniques in helping humans to play Eleusis.

In quite a different context, one of the aviation and space corporations used Eleusis in an advertisement for recruiting engineers and scientists. Here is a quote from their ad: "To win at Eleusis . . . requires the ability to form reasonable inductive hypotheses on minimal evidence and the willingness to abandon them in the face of contrary evidence. To win is to be flexible." The ad goes on to say that they are seeking to employ the scientist who is this type of strategist.

Another project involving Eleusis is being carried on by Donald Michie, a biologist in England, who is studying ways a machine could be programmed to learn Eleusis. He has previously done some interesting work with machines that can learn games and improve as they play, thus providing some insight into human learning.

I hope that by now I've aroused your curiosity as to what it is about Eleusis that created this interest. When you read the rules, though, you will find that the game is deceptively simple and that absolutely no mathematical or scientific knowledge is needed to play it. In fact, even after playing the game you will probably still ask what there is scientific about it. In order to answer this question, I have followed the game with a section of Notes on Eleusis that discuss its strategy and some of the philosophy behind the game. But I hasten to assure you that no one needs to read these notes in order to enjoy a game of Eleusis. I recommend them only if you are interested in the mental processes involved in playing the game.

General Description

THE OBJECT OF THE GAME is to get rid of as many cards as you can by playing them on the "starter pile" in the center of the table. The unusual feature of Eleusis is that for every new hand of play there is a different rule governing what cards may be played on the starter pile. And at the beginning of the play none of the players know what the rule is.

This secret rule is made up by the dealer, who does not take part in the play. The dealer does not tell the players what his rule is; but every time a player puts a card on the starter pile, the dealer says whether the card played conforms to his rule or not. If the dealer says the card is right, then the player may leave it on the starter pile. If the dealer says the card is wrong, the player must take it back.

Each player will try to reason out what the dealer's secret rule is by observing what cards are accepted on the starter pile and what cards are rejected. Once a player has a good idea of what the rule is, he will know what cards he can play and what cards he cannot play, and thus he will be able to get rid of his cards faster.

**Typical
Layout
for
Eleusis**

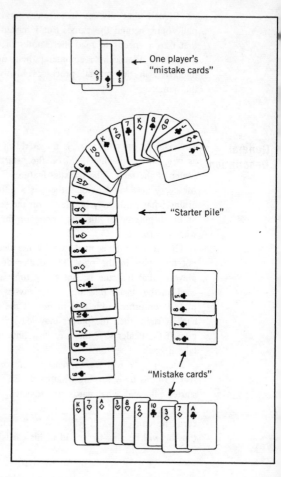

← One player's "mistake cards"

← "Starter pile"

"Mistake cards"

**The
Deal**

A STANDARD PACK of 52 cards is used. Before starting the game, it may be necessary to remove a number of cards from the pack so that each hand will receive the same amount. If there are three playing the game (including the dealer), one card should be removed; if there are

76

four playing, no cards are removed; if five are playing, three cards are removed; if six are playing, one card is removed; if seven are playing, three cards are removed; and if eight are playing, two cards are removed. It does not matter which cards are taken out, but the ♠A must remain in the deck.

The remaining cards are cut for deal; the player drawing the lowest card is dealer. Cards are ranked with ace low, and those of the same number are ranked spade, heart, diamond, club. The deal passes to the left after each hand.

The dealer takes no cards for himself. He deals out the entire deck to the other players, except for the last card, which he places face up in the center of the table. This is the "starter" card.

The Secret Rule

THE DEALER now makes up his secret rule that will govern what cards can be played on the starter pile. An example of a rule he might make up is this: "If the top card of the starter pile is red, a black card must be played; and if the top card is black, a red card must be played." Another rule might be: "If the top card is a spade, play a heart; if the top card is a heart, play a diamond; if the top card is a diamond, play a club; and if the top card is a club, play a spade." At the end of these directions there are several more examples of rules. This list should give you other ideas as to what sort of rules you can make up. The rules in the list are ranked approximately from the simplest to the most complicated.

As you will see later, the dealer will score a certain amount during the hand. The scoring is set up so that the dealer will score more if one of the players is getting rid of his cards faster than the others. One player will get ahead of the others if he has figured out the dealer's rule and the others haven't. Therefore the strategy for the dealer is this: He should judge the abilities of the players as to how complicated a rule each can figure out. Then he should make up a rule that is complicated enough so that all the players will not figure it out in the early stages of the game; but the rule should also be simple enough so that one player, or at most two players, will have it figured out early in the game.

If your group is playing this game for the first time, it will work out better if the dealer makes up a very simple rule. And beginning dealers should guard against the tendency to underestimate the difficulty of the rules they make up.

After the dealer has decided on a rule, he writes it down on a piece of paper and folds the paper over. None of the players are to see what he has written until the hand is over.

The Play, First Stage

THE PLAYER whose hand contains the ace of spades plays first. He picks any card from his hand (not necessarily the ♠A) and places it on the starter card in the center of the table. The dealer then says whether this card conforms to his rule or not. If the dealer says, "Right," the player leaves his card in the center. If the dealer says, "Wrong," the player must remove his card and place it face up in front of him. The turn passes to the left, and, when the first player has his turn again, he plays another card from his hand.

The cards that a player has face up in front of him are called his "mistake cards." During this first stage of the play when they still have cards in their hands, the players may not use any of their mistake cards. A player's mistake cards should be fanned out so that each card is visible. The cards should overlap, with the last card played on top, as in the illustration of a typical layout on page 76.

The cards that are accepted in the center of the table form the starter pile. These cards must be kept in the order played, and they also should be fanned out to make each card visible.

A player must play a card each time it is his turn, even if he thinks the card will be wrong.

The Dealer's Score

WHEN NO PLAYER has any more cards in his hand, the first stage of the play is ended. At this point the dealer's score is figured. His score is based on how far the leading player is ahead of the other players. The leading player at this point is the one who has the least number of mistake cards in front of him. If two or more players are tied for having the fewest mistake cards, pick one of them and call him the "leading" player for the purpose of scoring here.

If there are two players plus the dealer in the game, the dealer's score is the number of mistake cards the leading player has, subtracted from the number of mistake cards the other player has. (In all scoring, the values of the cards are not considered, only how many there are.)

If the game consists of three players plus the dealer, to find the dealer's score you count the number of mistake cards the leading player has, multiply this by 2, and then subtract this number from the number of mistake cards both the other players have.

If there are four players and the dealer, multiply the number of mistake cards the leading player has by 3 and subtract this from the number of cards the other three players have.

For five players plus dealer, the multiplier is 4; for six, the multiplier is 5; and so on.

As an example, suppose there are three players and the dealer. *A* has 10 mistake cards in front of him, *B* has 5 mistake cards, and *C,* the leading player, has 3 mistake cards. The number of cards the leading player has is multiplied by 2, which gives 6. The sum of *A*'s and *B*'s cards is 15. The 6 is subtracted from the 15 to give 9. The dealer therefore scores 9 points.

The dealer's score is recorded, and the player who has the next turn starts the second stage of the play.

The Play, Second Stage

THE PLAYERS use their mistake cards during this stage. The mistake cards are still kept face up so they can be seen by everyone, but instead of keeping them in order, a player may rearrange them any time he wishes. In his turn, a player places one of his mistake cards on top of the starter pile, and the dealer again says whether the card is right or wrong. If the card is wrong, the player removes it and puts it back face up among his other mistake cards.

As before, you must play a card each time it is your turn. You cannot play a previously rejected card unless another card has been accepted on the starter pile since the last time you played the card (or unless you have no other cards you can play).

The hand ends when one player goes out by getting rid of all his cards; or it ends when the dealer sees that it is impossible for any more cards to be accepted on the starter pile.

When the hand is ended, the players may look and see what rule the dealer has written down. After the scores are figured, all the cards are shuffled together to be dealt by the player to the left of the previous dealer.

Scoring

A PLAYER figures his score for a hand as follows: He takes the number of cards he holds, multiplies it by the number of players there are besides himself and the dealer, and then subtracts this number from the number of cards that are held by the other players.

A bonus of 6 points is given to the player who went out. If no one went out, the bonus is given to the player who had the least number of cards at the end. If two or more players are tied for having the least number of cards, they divide the bonus among themselves.

If a player's score for the hand comes out to be minus, he scores zero for the hand.

The following is an example of scoring: There are four players besides the dealer. *A* has got rid of all his cards, *B* has 2 cards left, *C* has 3 cards, and *D* has 10 cards.

A scores 15 points for the cards that the other players have. Since he has no cards himself, he does not subtract anything. And since he went out, he scores the 6-point bonus. His score is therefore 21 points.

B adds up the number of cards the other three players have and gets 13. From this he subtracts the number of cards he himself has times three, since there are three players besides himself and the dealer: 2 times 3 is 6, and 6 subtracted from 13 is 7. *B* therefore scores 7 points.

C's score is figured out to be 3 points.

If *D's* score were figured, it would come out to be minus 25. *D* therefore scores nothing on this hand.

The scores of the players and the score of the dealer are recorded for each hand. Each person's score is added to his scores for the previous hands.

The game continues until each person has been dealer once. After the last player has completed his deal and the hand has ended, the one who has the highest game score is the winner.

Miscellaneous Rules

IF A PLAYER makes no mistakes and gets rid of all his cards before some of the other players have even played all the cards in their hands, then the players lay down the cards in their hands, and these cards are counted among their mistake cards. The scores for the dealer and the players are figured at this point in the usual way.

The dealer may not use a rule under which, for a majority of the turns, less than one-fifth of the cards would be called right when played on the starter pile. For example, the following rule: "Play a card whose number is one unit higher than the top card" is unacceptable, since at each turn only four cards out of the entire deck could be played.

Unless the dealer states otherwise in his rule, the following conventions will be followed:

If a rule is not applicable until more than one card is on the starter pile, then the first player is right no matter what he plays.

If the rule involves numbers, the ace is worth 1, the jack is worth 11, queen is worth 12, and king is worth 13. If it is to be permissible to "turn the corner," that is, to have the following sequence, J-Q-K-A-2-3, the dealer must state so in his rule.

Anything is permissible that is not prohibited in a rule. For example, if the rule says only, "If the top card is red, play a black," then it is assumed that if the top card is black, anything can be played.

After the dealer has written down his rule, he may, if he wishes, give a hint as to what it is. For instance, he might say, "This rule involves red and black and odd and even," or "This rule involves the top two cards of the starter pile." After the play has commenced, the dealer is not allowed to give any further hints (unless, of course, you are playing very informally).

It is usually convenient for the new dealer to write his rule down on the same piece of paper the previous dealer used. If you play this game often, you might find it a good idea for the host to keep a book of blank pages for the rules to be written in. Each dealer can sign his name to his rule and perhaps record any hint he gave and what score he made. This will give the host a collection of various rules.

SOME PLAYERS PREFER to deal out two decks instead of one. They find that this allows more involved play, especially when there are more than four players.

When two decks are used, one of the ♠A should be among the cards removed. It will then be possible to determine who plays first with the remaining one.

Examples of Secret Rules

THE FOLLOWING are some examples of rules that might give you some ideas or which you might use as they are:

1. If the top card of the starter pile is red, play a black; if it is black, play a red.

2. On the starter pile, a diamond must be followed by a club, which must be followed by a heart, which must be followed by a spade, which must be followed by a diamond.

3. If top card is odd, play an even; if even, play an odd.

4. If the top card is among the cards ace to 7, play a card among 8 to K; and if the card is among 8 to K, play a card A to 7.

5. The number of the card played must be one, two, or three units higher than the number of the top card. The numbers may turn the corner.

6. If the top card is even, play a red card; if the top card is odd, play a black card.

7. If top card is red, play a card A to 7; if black, play a card 8 to K.

8. If the top card is of a lower number than the card under it, play a card of a higher number than the top card; and if the top card is of a higher number than the card under it, play a card of a lower number than the top card. The first player is correct unless he plays a card equal in number to the starter card.

9. The card played must be of the same suit or of the same number as the top card.

10. Divide the number of the top card by 4; if you get a remainder of 1, play a spade; if you get a remainder of 2, play a heart; if you get a remainder of 3, play a diamond; and if you get no remainder, play a club.

NOTES ON ELEUSIS

AS PROMISED, I'll try to explain the scientific interest that has centered on Eleusis.

The major attraction of Eleusis has been the fact that it is one of the very few games that involve inductive reasoning. Most games call for deductive reasoning on the part of the players. In making a choice of what move to make in a game, a player is presented with a given set of rules and a given situation. His problem is to deduce what new situations would result from the various moves available to him.

In Eleusis the thinking runs in the opposite direction. The players are able to observe what specific situations result from various moves made in the game, but their problem is to discover the general rule that governs these situations. For at the start of each new hand of Eleusis, one of the rules of the game is unknown to the players.

This formulation of a general rule to explain a set of specific observations is precisely what inductive reasoning is. This same reasoning is the basis of all creative scientific thought, it is perhaps the basis of much creative thought in general, and it certainly plays a large part in everyday reasoning. Eleusis affords a clear view of this process at work; and players of the game should discover some fascinating, and often inexplicable, mental abilities within themselves.

Eleusis was derived from a series of psychological experiments designed to study inductive reasoning, or what was referred to psychologically as "concept-formation." An example of these experiments is one in which the experimenter shows a series of cards with drawings of flowers on them. The person being shown the cards tells how he thinks the flowers are similar; for example, he might say they all have three leaves. Three-leaved-ness is then the concept he thinks unites them. In another experiment the subject might be asked to pick out cards of flowers that will fit into the same category as certain flowers already shown to him. Different conditions of the experiments can be varied, and the performance of the person taking the experiment will vary. In this way some knowledge can be gained as to how this thought process operates and what factors influence it.

As you can recognize, I changed little when I transformed these experiments into a game. The major change is that the concept (or secret rule) involves the relation between the cards in the pile instead of it being inherent in each card, as in the experiments. Also, a system of scoring was devised that usually rewards the player who discovered the concept and which encourages the dealer to use concepts that are discoverable and will make a good game. However, even with these changes the game tests the abilities of the players at inductive reasoning in the same way as the experiments test this ability. In fact, for purposes of study, Eleusis even has some advantages over the experiments. Every psychological experiment has the problem of creating enough motivation to make its findings meaningful; in a game, however, players are competing against each other, and there is hardly ever a lack of motivation.

One thing that can be learned both from the experiments and from Eleusis is that individuals vary greatly in their concept-forming ability. Some will play their first game of Eleusis expertly, while others will never catch on to it. It can also be noted that concept-formation is a mental factor that is very distinct from other factors. I have known people of very high general intelligence who were brilliant in other games but could not play Eleusis at all. And I have played it with twelve-year-olds who could beat any adult in the group.

In addition to the interest in the psychology involved in playing Eleusis, there was also a certain philosophical interest in the game. This is because Eleusis, besides evoking a player's ability to discover a general truth, also provides an analogy to "truth" itself.

In attempting to discover the secret rule, the best strategy a player can use is to form various hypotheses about the rule and then test these hypotheses by the cards he plays. By retaining certain hypotheses and rejecting others, the player will be able to work out a theory to explain the ordering of the cards on the starter pile. This strategy is basically equivalent to the scientific method.

If the players are thought of as scientists, the dealer's secret rule may be thought of as a law of nature they are attempting to discover. The game then becomes a useful model for clarifying certain questions about what actually are laws of nature and theories. Such philosophical discusion gets to be a little out of place in a game book, but if the reader is interested in this analogy, I refer him to *The 2nd Scientific American Book of Mathematical Puzzles & Diversions,* by Martin Gardner. Gardner wrote the original article on Eleusis in *Scientific American,* and his book contains a complete discussion of this analogy along with a deftly humorous account of how the various schools of philosophy would interpret a game of Eleusis.

NOTES ON STRATEGY

I HAVE AVOIDED any extensive discussion of strategy in the description of the other games in the book, since one of the enjoyable features of a new game is the fact that its strategies are unknown and the players have the challenge of discovering them. A book that tells how to win as well as how to play a new game takes away some of this challenge.

However, since Eleusis has been played for some time now, I think it would be of interest to open a discussion of its strategy. I should caution you, though, that you will probably find this discussion dull unless you have already played a few games of Eleusis.

The important problem is, of course, how the player is to discover the dealer's secret rule. The ability to form concepts seems to be something a player either has or does not have, and it may be that learning does not have much effect on increasing this ability.

It would seem, then, that the prospects are poor for a player improving his game, especially since concept-formation is a nebulous, creative sort of process that has not been well analyzed by psychology. About the best advice psychology can offer on the subject is, as in general problem-solving, for the player not to get a "set." Often a player will have one idea of what the secret rule can be. He will play a card to try out this idea; and, if it does not work, he won't discard the idea but will keep trying it again or trying ideas very similar to it. A player may, for example, get the set that the secret rule involves suits. After trying out several hypotheses that involve suits, he will not go on to try something involving numbers but will continue with suits.

In avoiding set, you should avoid placing any unnecessary restrictions upon yourself, such as, "The rule must involve suits," or, "The rule must involve odd and even cards," or, "The rule involves only the top card of the pile." The more fluid your thinking is, the greater number of ideas you try, and the greater the difference there is among these ideas,- the more likely you will be to hit the correct rule.

There is, however, in addition to this psychological advice, a systematic method that will enable a player to discover a large number of secret rules. Most secret rules are of a pattern such as these examples:

"If the top card of the pile is red, play an odd card; if it is black, play even."

"If top card is odd, play a card 8 to K; if even, play a card A to 7."

"If the top card is red, play a card higher than the top card; if it is black, play a card lower than the top card."

Note that each of these rules has two variables. The first variable involves the top card of the pile; and the second variable involves the card to be played. Notice that the variables involve what may be called different dimensions. For example, in the first rule above, the first variable involves the "red-black" dimension, and the second variable involves the "odd-even" dimension. These dimensions can be described as absolute or relative; for instance the "8 to K − A to 7" dimension is absolute, whereas the "higher than − lower than" dimension is relative. The relative dimensions are of course harder to see. A player should keep in mind and try out as many dimensions as possible.

In using this method, the player first attempts to discover the second variable of the secret rule, the variable that involves the card played. In doing this, he should not concern himself too much with the starter pile as a whole, but he should observe mainly the mistake cards. When a card is called wrong, it should be compared with whatever card is next called right. For each comparison that he makes, the player may be able to eliminate one or more dimensions that the second variable could not involve.

For example, suppose the first card of the starter pile is a ♠K. One player plays a ♡2 and the dealer calls this wrong. The next player plays a ◊J and this is called right. A player should now make a comparison between the ♡2 and the ◊J. One thing he will notice is that both cards are red. Since the ♡2 may not follow the ♠K, but the ◊J, another red card, may follow the ♠K, he can deduce that red-black is probably not the dimension involved in the second variable of the secret rule. Whenever the rejected card and the accepted card show no change along a certain dimension, that dimension can probably be discarded as the one involved in the second variable. However, when the rejected and accepted cards do vary in certain dimensions, one of these dimensions that have not previously been rejected may be the one involved in the second variable. Notice that the ♡2 and the ◊J do show change along the odd-even, the high-low, and other dimensions. These dimensions are therefore retained for consideration.

Suppose in the same example that the next card played is a ♡3 which is called wrong, the next card is a ♣J which is also called wrong, and then a ♣4 is played which is called right. Comparisons should now be made between the ♡3 and the ♣4, and between the ♣J and the ♣4. Since the ♡3 and the ♣4 are both low cards we can discard the high-low dimension. And since the ♣J and the ♣4 are both clubs we can assume that the dimension of suits is not involved. However, since both rejected cards are odd and the accepted card is even, we can retain the hypothesis that the dimension involved is odd-even.

Suppose the next card is a ♣9, which is rejected, and then an ♡8, which is accepted. When we compare these two cards we cannot dispose of any other simple dimensions; however the comparison is another confirming instance of our hypothesis that odd-even is the dimension involved. In fact, since we have discarded all the other common dimensions, we can now assume with a high degree of certainty that odd-even is the second variable of the secret rule. Our perception now of the secret rule is this: "If the top card is x, play an odd card; and if it is y, play an even card." x-y represents the first variable which we still do not know.

Even though we know only half the secret rule, we now have enough information to make rational plays on certain occasions. If it were now our turn, we would not know what card to play on the ♡8. However, suppose it is another player's turn, he plays a ♠6, and the dealer calls it wrong. We now know that we can play any odd card and it will be called right.

After the second variable of the secret rule has been discovered, it is usually an easier matter to find the first. This can probably best be done by looking back over the entire starter pile. Suppose that in our example a few additional plays were made and the starter pile grew to this: ♠K ◇J ♣4 ♡8 ♣3 ◇2 ♣Q ♣2 ♣10 ♡10 ♠A. As you can see the first variable must be more complicated than the second since none of the common dimensions seem to work for it. A more systematic approach would be mentally to divide these cards into two classes, those that precede odd cards and those that precede even cards. The two classes would look like this:

Preceding odd: ♠K ♡8 ♡10

Preceding even: ◇J ♣4 ♣3 ◇2 ♣Q ♣2 ♣10

On examining the first group we see that it contains both red and black cards, so red-black cannot be the dimension. All the cards in the first group are high cards, so high-low could be a possible dimension. However, we see that the second group has both high and low cards, so we have to reject high-low as the dimension. Odd and even are distributed among both groups, so this dimension is also rejected. One possibility we can see though is that the first group is made up entirely of spades and hearts, and the second group contains only diamonds and clubs. We can therefore make the following as our hypothesis for what the secret rule is: "If the top card is a spade or heart, play an odd card; if the top card is a diamond or club, play an even."

Since this hypothesis has worked in a number of instances so far, it is probable that we have correctly figured out the secret rule. In any event we would assume the truth of our hypothesis and play accordingly. If a play in the future contradicts the hypothesis, we would have to re-examine it, seeing whether it should be discarded or whether it can be modified to include the new circumstance. Sometimes, even, a player may realize that his hypothesis is wrong, but he still may find it valuable if it continues to work in a large percentage of plays.

The method I have outlined here works best when the secret rule is similar to the examples given on page 88. However, it is possible to generalize this method to discover other types of rules.

It will work with one-dimensional rules such as, "If the top card is odd, play an even; if the top is even, play an odd." These rules can usually be discovered faster, though, by studying the starter pile as a whole, since they create a clear pattern on the pile. A player should of course watch the entire starter pile to see if it develops any peculiar characteristics that will give a hint as to the rule.

Often the secret rule will have two variables, but the first variable will not be involved exclusively with the top card of the pile. Two examples of these rules are, "If the card second from the top of the starter pile is even, play a red; if it is odd, play a black," and, "If the two top cards of the pile are similar in color, play an even; if they are dissimilar, play an odd." The method I described will quickly uncover the second variable in these rules, but the player will have to look around quite a bit for the first variable.

The following, however, are some rules that completely defy analysis by this method:

"If the card played is red, it must be higher than the top card of the starter pile; if it is black, it must be lower than the top card."

"If the last player made a correct choice, play a red; and if he made an incorrect choice, play a black."

"If you were the first or third to play, always play a card of the same color as the top card of the pile; if you were the second or fourth to play, always play a card of different color than the top card of the pile."

One good feature of Eleusis is that it can never become too routine because of the discovery of too perfect a strategy; for the dealer can always make up rules that are more complicated than the strategy.

Since the method described here cannot always be relied upon, the player will have to judge at what point to abandon it during a hand and look for other ways of analyzing the cards. What methods he uses are strictly personal, and we are again at the psychological question of what is involved in this reasoning.

Sometimes players will get inexplicable "hunches" that will lead them to the correct rule. Others have noticed that if they relax while playing the game, they may suddenly see a pattern that they could not discover by systematic analysis.

There is even the possibility that in games of Eleusis a player may get certain insights into his own process of inductive reasoning, or perhaps even discover ways he can improve that reasoning.

CHAPTER VIII

CONSTRUCTION

**For
Two
Players**

CITY PLANNERS have often wondered why anyone would want to drive to work every day. A lot of motorists could answer: it's the sport of the thing!

What greater thrill than to take your car out in the morning and plot a new route to the office. And when you find the new route is blocked by as many cars as the other routes you've tried, what fun you'll have on the trip home, again trying to find a way around the congestion. How your heart leaps up when plans for a new expressway are announced. For one foolish moment you think the game is won. But no; the highway opens and it attracts even more commuters, until it too is clogged with automobiles.

Well, all these delightful moments, and more, can be experienced in a game of Construction, and you don't even have to leave home.

In Construction your object is to build a road of cards that will enable you to move a piece, called a commuter, out a certain number of spaces from your home base and then back onto it. The excitement, however, comes after you have constructed a road. Before you can move your commuter across it, you find your opponent, diabolical fiend that he is, has already been able to move a man onto the road to block you. This forces you to build an alternate route, but like as not, your unrelenting opponent will send men to block that path, too. You then counter, as is only just, by sending men to block your opponent's commuter or perhaps to block the paths of his men. Pretty soon a traffic jam of monumental proportions will have been created. At this point in the game many players, unfortunately, let their frustrations get the better of them; they kick over the table and go back to Gin Rummy. But if you persevere, you will find that ultimate triumph is possible: your commuter may be the first to make it back home.

A unique feature of Construction is that the network of roads over which the pieces move will grow as the game progresses. This causes one difficulty, though: before a game is halfway over, it will have outgrown the proportions of an ordinary bridge table. The game, therefore, should be played on a larger surface, such as a dining-room table or, possibly, the floor.

I hope you aren't discouraged by the length of these instructions or the size of some of the diagrams. The basic principles behind Construction are quite simple, although the players may use them to create complex situations. Once you've learned the details of the game, you'll find a handy summary of the rules on page 118.

A Typical Layout for Construction

(The stock and discard piles may be placed anywhere)

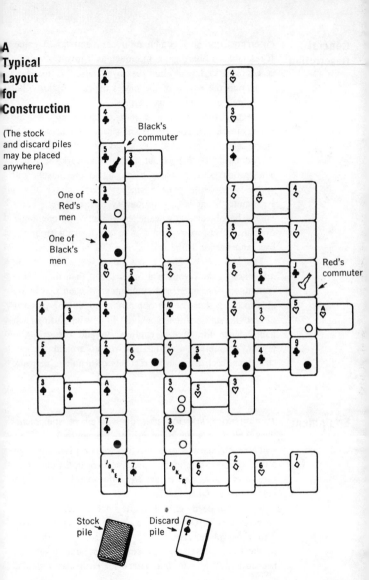

Black's commuter

One of Red's men

One of Black's men

Red's commuter

Stock pile

Discard pile

**General
Description**

CONSTRUCTION is a combination card and board game. It resembles a board game inasmuch as it involves moving pieces over a layout; but the layout itself is made of cards, and the moves of the pieces depend on cards that are turned up from the stock pile.

Creating the layout is a part of the game. As the players place cards on the playing surface, the layout takes shape, and it grows as the game goes on.

The cards in the layout form a network of roads. These roads start at bases belonging to the players and spread across the playing surface. Each player has a "commuter" that begins its journey at the player's home base. The object of the game is to move the commuter over the roads to a point ten spaces forward from the base and then to bring it back.

The players also have pieces called "men," which can move across the layout at a faster speed than that of the commuters. The men and commuters of each player are able to block those of the opponent, and shifting patterns of blocking and counter-blocking will develop during each game. Since the players continue to add cards to the layout, attempting to build new routes around the obstructions, each game will create its own unique network of roads.

Equipment

THOUGH CONSTRUCTION uses quite a bit of equipment, these objects can be found around the house.

Three standard decks and two jokers (158 cards in all) are used. (You might purchase three decks of miniature cards and use them. Miniature cards make the layout more manageable.)

Next you need several round, flat objects, such as checker men, poker chips, etc., to be used as men. The men of one player should all be of one color, and the men of the other player another color. The number of men needed is not definite, but sixteen for each player should be enough. However, it is best to have more on hand.

Finally, each player needs one object that is to be his commuter. The commuter should be distinct from the men. Two objects such as Chess kings, small bottles, or spools of thread can be used. It is best if the commuter of each player is of a color similar to the color of his men.

Preliminary

THE TWO JOKERS are laid down in this manner:

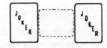

The distance between them should equal the length of a card. The two jokers are to be the two bases for the players. The players decide who is to use which base, and then each places his commuter on his own base.

The three decks are shuffled together and placed face down to form the stock pile.

The Play

THERE ARE NO HANDS in Construction. Instead, cards are turned up from the stock pile, and each card is played before the next is turned up.

The players do not take alternate turns; instead, one plays all the red cards (hearts and diamonds) that come up, and the other plays all the black cards (spades and clubs). Before the game starts, the players decide who is to play each color. If possible, the color of the cards a player plays should be similar to the color of his men. For example, if red and blue poker chips are used as men, then the player who is using the red chips should play the red cards, and the player who is using the blue chips should play the black cards.

Throughout the rest of these directions the player who has chosen to play the red cards is called "Red," and his opponent is called "Black."

The play proceeds in this manner: The top card of the stock pile is turned face up. It does not matter who picks up this top card. Whatever arrangement is most convenient for the players determines who picks up the cards from the stock pile.

If the card taken from the stock pile is red, it is given to Red to play. If the card is black, it is given to Black.

The player who has received the card then has four choices of what to do with it:

1. He may use the card for construction. In this case he adds the card to one of the roads (as explained in the section **"Rules Governing Construction"**).

2. He may use it to move his commuter. In this case he places the card on the discard pile and is thereby given the power to move his commuter one space (in accordance with the rules given in the section **"How a Commuter is Moved"**).

3. He may use it to move one of his men. In this case he places the card on the discard pile and moves a man one, two, or three spaces (in accordance with the rules given in the section **"How a Man is Moved"**).

4. He may "pass." In this case he places his card on the discard pile and does nothing else.

After the player has gotten rid of the card in one of these four ways, either player picks up the next card of the stock pile, and the same procedure is followed.

There is one exception: whenever a red *king* is turned up from the stock, Red brings a man onto the layout, and whenever a black *king* turns up, Black brings a man onto the layout. (This is further explained in the section **"How a Man is Brought Into Play."**) A king cannot be used for any other purpose.

When the stock pile is depleted, the discard pile is turned over, shuffled, and used as a new stock pile.

IF A PLAYER DECIDES to use a card for construction, he places that card on the layout next to a card that has previously been placed there or next to one of the jokers. The cards are laid face up, and one card may not be laid on top of another.

Since the object of the game is to move the commuter ten spaces forward from its base and then back onto its base, the players will usually start the game by building roads straight forward from their bases.

Thus the first card to be a part of your road will be placed end to end with the joker, the next card will be placed end to end to this first one, and so on. The diagram below shows a typical situation that results after a few cards have been laid down and after some moves have been made by the pieces. Notice that Red has played a ♡Q on Black's road, and Black has played a ♣10 on

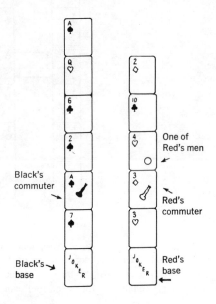

Red's road. As will be seen later, a player can hinder his opponent by adding high cards to the opponent's road.

In the diagram, Red has been able to bring one of his men onto the layout and has that man on the ♡4. If there were a card connecting the two roads, Red might be able to move his man over to his opponent's road. The diagram below shows how a card can be laid making the connection, and it shows Red moving his man into the path of Black's commuter.

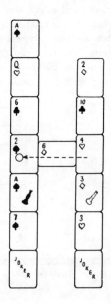

Black now has to work out a different way for his commuter to proceed forward. The following diagram shows one way he might construct a detour and move his commuter around the Red man.

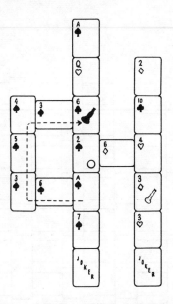

More roads would be added to this example as other situations came up. After a while the layout might look something like the typical layout on page 95. There you will notice some sort of pattern. It is necessary that the layout grow in an orderly fashion; thus players may not put cards down in a random manner but only in conformity with the overall pattern. This overall pattern is shown in the diagram on page 102. Cards may be laid only in spaces that correspond to spaces in this diagram.

The rules governing road-building can be summarized this way: *A card used for construction may be placed face up in any space corresponding to a space in the diagram on page 102, provided that the space is empty and that it is adjacent to a card that has previously been laid down or is adjacent to one of the jokers.*

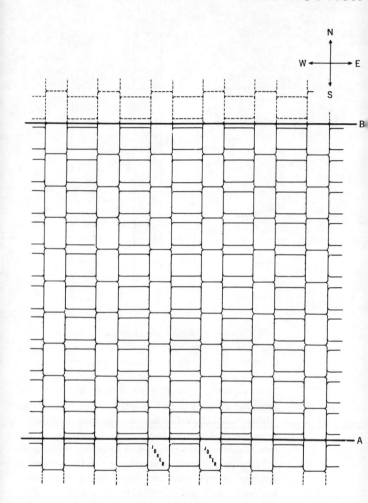

Diagram of all the possible places in which cards may be laid in Construction
This diagram can be extended indefinitely in any direction. Only in rare
instances would cards be laid in the spaces indicated by the dotted lines.

Be sure to note that when a card is placed *to the side* of a vertical card, the card is placed *horizontal* (and, conversely, a card placed to the side of a horizontal card is laid vertical).

Also notice the gap between a horizontal card and the card above or below it. Commuters and men may not move over this gap. For example, the commuter on the ♡ 3 in the diagram below could not move onto the ◇ A without first moving across the ♡ 5 and ♡ 2 or across the ♣ 3 and ♠ 4.

THE OBJECT OF THE GAME may now be stated more precisely with the aid of the diagram on page 102. The object is to move your commuter by any route and over any roads up onto any of the spaces that are immediately south of line *B,* and then to move it by any route over any roads back onto your joker. That is, you are to move your commuter to a point ten spaces north of your joker — but any number of spaces to the east or west — and then back onto the joker. The first player to accomplish this is the winner.

It is not necessary to build a road straight forward ten spaces from your joker. In fact, you might not even need

to build any road up to line *B,* for you can move your
commuter on roads that your opponent has built. You
may also move your commuter back on your opponent's
side of the layout and cross over his base to get back
to your own.

Blocking

THE RULES FOR BLOCKING are as follows: As long as a
Red man or the Red commuter occupies any of the
spaces north of line *A* in the diagram on page 102, none
of the Black men nor the Black commuter can move onto
or over this space. It makes no difference, however, how
many Red men occupy the same space with each other
or with the Red commuter. The rules apply equally, of
course, for Black.

An exception is made with the spaces south of line *A*
(on the "baseline"). There the men and commuters lose
their blocking power, and any number of one player's
men or his commuter can occupy the same space with any
number of his opponent's men or commuter. The purpose
of this exception is to make it unlikely that a commuter
will become hopelessly blocked from its base.

**How
a
Commuter
Is
Moved**

IF YOU DECIDE to use a card to move your commuter, you
place that card on the discard pile and then move your
commuter from the card it is on to an adjacent one.
However, you may not move your commuter onto a card
that has a higher value than the one you placed on the
discard pile. For this purpose the cards are evaluated
as follows:

A—	1	7—	7
2—	2	8—	8
3—	3	9—	9
4—	4	10—	10
5—	5	J—	10
6—	6	Q—	10
	joker—	10	

Note that the ten, jack, queen, and joker all have the same value. In order to move onto your opponent's joker, or to move onto your own joker at the end of the game, you need to discard a ten, a jack, or a queen. Kings have no numerical value, as they cannot be used for construction or to move pieces.

A commuter cannot move onto a card where it is blocked by one of the opponent's pieces.

The following is an example of how a commuter is moved. Suppose you are the Red player, and your commuter is in the following position:

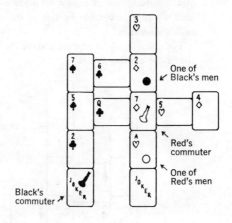

A ♢5 is turned up from the stock pile. If you wanted to use this card to move your commuter, you would place the card on the discard pile and you could then move your commuter onto the ♡5 or onto the ♡A. You could not move onto the ♣Q because it has a higher value than the ♢5 you placed on the discard pile. You could not move onto the ♢2 because it is occupied by one of Black's men.

Suppose instead that the card turned up from the stock

pile was a ♡ 10. If you discard it, you could move your commuter onto the ♣ Q, the ♡ 5, or the ♡ A. In this case the card you discarded is equal in value to the ♣ Q.

**How
a
Man
Is
Moved**

IF YOU DECIDE to use a card to move one of your men, you place that card on the discard pile and move the man one, two, or three spaces. This movement can be made in any direction, in a straight or crooked path; but it can be made only over existing roads, it cannot be made onto or across a card that has a higher value than the card you discarded, and it cannot be made onto or across a card where it is blocked by one of the opponent's men or his commuter.

For example, again suppose you are the Red player and this is the existing layout:

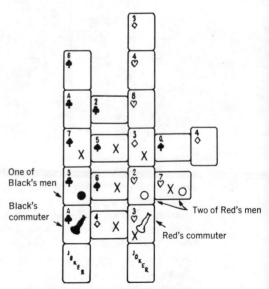

One of Black's men

Black's commuter

Two of Red's men

Red's commuter

A ♢7 is turned up from the stock pile. You take the card and decide to use it to move your man that is on the ♡2. You place the ♢7 on the discard pile, and then you can move this man onto any of the spaces marked with an *x*.

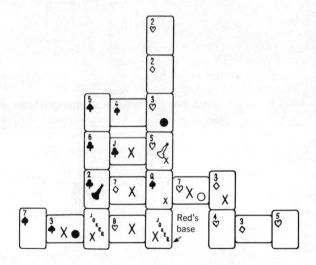

WHENEVER a black king is turned up from the stock pile, it is placed on the discard pile and Black immediately brings one of his men into play. When a red king is turned up, Red brings one of his men into play. When he brings a man into play, a player may either place it on his joker or he may immediately move it along existing roads one, two, or three spaces from the joker. This move cannot be made onto or over a card where the man is blocked by one of the opponent's pieces, but it does not matter what the values are of the cards moved on.

For example, if this is the existing layout:

and a ◇K is turned up, the king is placed on the discard pile and Red places one of his men on any one of the spaces marked with an *x*. (Notice the Black's man on the ♠3 has no blocking power since it is on the "base line.")

YOU MAY NOT trap your opponent's commuter between two of your men or between one of your men and your commuter. For example, as long as the Black commuter is in this position:

Miscellaneous Rules

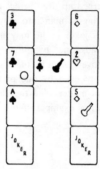

Red cannot move a man or his commuter onto the ♡2 unless he moves his man off the ♣7.

You also may not trap a commuter in the middle of four of your pieces, as in the following situation:

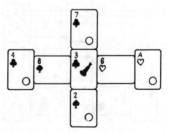

or in any similar situation such as:

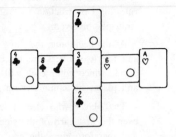

However, larger traps involving six or more men are permissible. It hasn't happened yet that both commuters become trapped, but if it does, the game is a draw.

A rare situation that might occur after extended play is one in which there are no cards of one color except for kings in the stock and discard piles. Whenever this is discovered, the players wait until the stock pile is depleted, and then each player removes ten cards of his color from the layout and places them on the discard pile. The players may remove only cards that have no men or commuters on them. The discard pile is then shuffled and used as a new stock pile.

If after more play the piles again have no cards of one color except kings, the procedure is repeated, except that this time the players take from the layout as many cards of their color as they wish. This second procedure may be repeated any number of times.

Sample Game

THE FOLLOWING DESCRIBES the opening portion of a fairly typical game. This description should help clarify the rules of Construction as well as indicate some of the strategies involved.

At the beginning, the three decks are shuffled together, and the two jokers are placed in position. The players decide which color each will use; each chooses his base and places his commuter on it.

The player who elected to play the red cards turns over the first card of the stock. He sees that it is a ♠, and therefore gives the card to Black. Black places the card in front of his joker, thereby starting a road from his base. Red turns up the next card, which is a ◇ Q. It is his card to play, and he decides to add it to Black's road. He therefore places it in front of the ♠ 5. (It's easier to visualize this game if you refer to the diagram ahead.)

Black turns up the next card, a ♣ J, which Black places in front of Red's base. Black then turns up the next card, an ♡ 8. Red feels that this card is too high to put on his own road, but it's not high enough to act as a hindrance if he put it on Black's road. He doesn't see any other way he could use it; so he places it on the table to start the discard pile and says, "I pass."

From this point on, for simplicity's sake, the card that is turned up from the stock will be written at the left followed by a description of how the card was played.

♣ 8 Black decides to use this card to move his commuter. He therefore places the ♣ 8 on the discard pile and moves his commuter one space forward, onto the ♠ 5.

♡ 2 Red adds this to his road in front of the ♣ J.

♠ 3 Black places this in front of the ◇ Q.

◇ A Added to Red's road.

◇ 3 Also added to Red's road.

At this point the layout appears as follows:

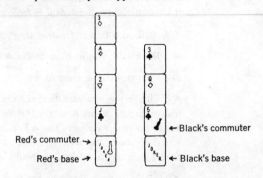

♡K Having this turn up entitles Red to bring a man onto the layout. He discards the king and decides to move this man the full three spaces from his base. He therefore places the man on the ◇A.

♡4 Red decides to use this card for construction and places it horizontally between the ◇A and the ♠3, as is shown below:

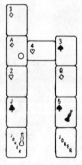

With the ♡4 in this position, Red might be able to move his man onto the ♠3 or the ◇Q and thus block the path of Black's commuter.

♡3 Red cannot use this card to move his man onto the

♠ 3, since he has to move over the ♡ 4. Instead he uses it for construction and adds it in front of the ◇ 3.

◇ A Red adds this in front of the ♡ 3.

♣ 5 Black adds this in front of the ♠ 3.

◇ 2 Red adds this in front of the ◇ A.

◇ 8 This is the first card that enables Red to move his man where he wants it to go. He discards the ◇ 8 and moves his man over onto the ♠ 3. Red would have preferred to move the man onto the ◇ Q, but he would need a card of the value of ten to do so.

♠ 9 Black discards this and passes.

♠ 10 Black discards this and moves his commuter forward onto the ◇ Q.

♠ 4 Black places this card on the layout between the ♡ 2 and the ◇ Q, as shown here:

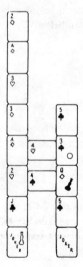

Black's plan is to move his commuter over to the road Red has built and then proceed forward on it.

◇7 Red discards this and passes.

♣4 Black uses this to move his commuter onto the ♠4.

♣8 Black moves his commuter to the ♡2.

♡Q Red sees that Black is about to proceed forward on Red's road; he therefore uses the ♡Q to move his man back onto the ◇A.

♠5 Black's commuter is blocked from moving forward on Red's road; so he moves back toward his own road. He discards the ♠5 and moves his commuter onto the ♠4.

♠Q Black moves his commuter onto the ◇Q. The pieces are now in this position:

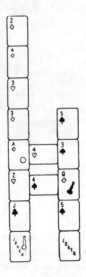

♠K This enables Black to bring a man onto the layout. He moves the man past his commuter and onto the ♠3. This Black man will keep the Red man from returning to the ♠3, and it thereby protects the commuter's path at this point.

◇K Red brings a man onto the layout and places it on the ♡2.

♣K Black brings another man onto the layout; however, this time he leaves the man on his base instead of moving it any place else, although he could have placed it on the ♠5, ◇Q, ♠3, or the ♠4.

♠7 Black places this card between the two jokers. The following is the layout at this point:

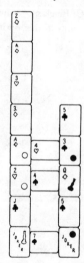

♠Q It now becomes apparent why Black left his man at his base. Black discards the ♠Q and moves the man from his base across the ♠7, across Red's base, and onto the ♣J. This man now blocks Red from proceeding forward from his base. Red's commuter was not able to block the Black man from coming across Red's base since the pieces lose their blocking power on the baseline.

◇6 Red uses this for construction and lays it horizontal to the left of his base.

◇4 Red places this card vertical and to the left of the ◇6.

♡8 Red uses this to move his commuter onto the ◇6.

♣2 Black lays this card horizontal and to the left of the ♣J, where he has his man.

♡5 Red places this card in front of the ◇4 and to the left of the ♣2.

◇4 Red uses this to move his commuter onto the ◇4 in the layout.

♣6 Black moves his man from the ♣J to the ♡5. The layout is now as follows:

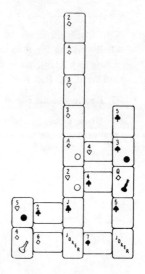

Red had tried to move his commuter to the left past the Black man, but Black was able to move his man over to prevent this.

♡ 10 Red now tries moving past Black's man by going to the right. He uses the ♡ 10 to move his commuter onto the ◇ 6.

◇ 9 Red cannot use this to move his commuter back onto his base; so instead he places it at the end of Black's road, in front of the ♣ 5.

◇ J Red moves his commuter onto his base.

♡ J Red moves his commuter onto the ♣ J.

♣ K Black moves a new man onto the ♠ 3.

♠ 5 Black moves his commuter onto the ♠ 3. Black now has three pieces on this ♠ 3.

♡ 8 The Red commuter moves onto the ♡ 2.

◇ 9 The Red commuter moves onto the ◇ A.

♣ 10 Black moves his man from the ♡ 5 back onto the ♣ J. By placing the man there, Black prevents Red from sending any additional men he may acquire straight forward from the Red base.

♡ 7 Red moves his commuter onto the ◇ 3.

♣ 6 Black moves his commuter onto the ♣ 5. The condition of the layout is now as follows:

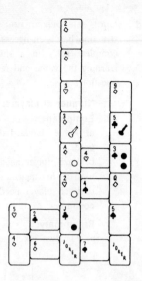

We will not follow the play in this sample game beyond this point. Since both commuters have moved in front of the men that could block them, they will probably be able to proceed up to line *B* without further hindrance. However, the return trip should be more complicated, because each commuter will have many more men to face. Often a player is able to position several men along a horizontal line in order to create a solid wall that will force the opponent's commuter on a wide detour.

In the average game of Construction, the men are usually not able to go into offensive action as early as they were in this sample game. However, each game played is quite different, depending on the opportunities for blocking and on the strategy used by the players. Some games are over in a short time, while others may take more than an hour and extend over a large area.

Condensed Rules

SINCE THE DESCRIPTION of the plays involved in Construction has been necessarily long, this section gives the complete rules in a shorter form for convenience in learning the game and referring back to specific rules as questions arise.

1. **Number of players:** Two.

2. **Equipment:**

   a. Three standard decks and two jokers are to be used.

   b. Each player needs sixteen or more objects to be used as his men.

   c. Each player needs one object to be used as his commuter.

3. **Preliminary:**

   a. The two jokers are laid down in this manner:

   at a distance apart equal to the length of a card.

   b. The players decide which of them is to use which joker as his base. Each player then places his commuter on his base.

   c. The players decide who is to play the red cards and who the black cards. Throughout these rules the one who chose the red cards is called "Red," and the one who chose the black cards is called "Black."

   d. The three decks are shuffled together to form the stock pile.

4. **The object of the game:** The winner of the game is the first player who moves his commuter up onto any of the spaces that are shown immediately south of line *B* in the diagram on page 102 and then moves his commuter back onto his base.

5. **The play:** The top card of the stock pile is turned up. If it is red, it is given to Red to play. If it is black, it is given to Black.

The player who has received the card then uses it in one of the following four ways (unless the card is a king):

(1) He may use it for construction.

(2) He may use it to move his commuter.

(3) He may use it to move one of his men.

(4) He may "pass."

When a player "passes," he places the card face up on the discard pile and says, "I pass."

Whenever the stock pile is depleted, the discard pile is turned over, shuffled, and used as a new stock pile.

6. **Rules governing construction:** If you have decided to use a card for construction, you lay that card face up in any space corresponding to a space in the diagram on page 102, provided the space is empty and provided it is adjacent to a card that has previously been laid down or is adjacent to one of the jokers.

7. **The values assigned to each card:**

A—	1	7—	7
2—	2	8—	8
3—	3	9—	9
4—	4	10—	10
5—	5	J—	10
6—	6	Q—	10
	joker—	10	

8. **Rules governing the moving of men and commuters:** When you decide to use a card to move your commuter, you place that card face up on the discard pile and move your commuter one space in any direction.

When you decide to use a card to move a man, you place that card face up on the discard pile and move one of your men one space, two spaces, or three spaces. This movement can be made in any direction, in a straight or crooked path. *However:*

a. You can move a man or commuter only onto or over space where cards have been laid down.

b. You cannot move a man or commuter onto a card or over any card that has a higher value than the card you put on the discard pile.

c. You cannot move a man or commuter onto or over any space north of line *A* in the diagram on page 102 if that space is occupied by one of your opponent's men or his commuter.

9. **How a man is brought into play:** Whenever a black king is turned up from the stock pile, it is placed on the discard pile and Black immediately brings one of his men into play. When a red king is turned up, Red brings one of his men into play. When he brings a man into play, a player may either place it on his joker or he may immediately move it along existing roads one, two, or three spaces from the joker. *However:*

a. You can move the man only onto or over space where cards have been laid down.

b. You cannot move the man onto or over any space north of line *A* if that space is occupied by one of your opponent's men or his commuter.

10. **Miscellaneous rules:** You may not trap your opponent's commuter between two of your pieces or in the middle of four of your pieces. (If both commuters are trapped by six or more pieces, the game is a draw.)

Whenever the players discover that there are no cards of one color except kings in the stock pile and discard pile, they wait until the stock pile is depleted, and then each player removes ten cards of his color from the layout and places them on the discard pile. The players may remove only cards that have no men or commuters on them. If after more play the piles again have no cards of one color except kings, the procedure is repeated, except that this time the players take from the layout as many cards of their color as they wish.

CHAPTER IX

ULTIMA

**For
Two
Players**

THIS IS NOT the ultimate in games, but it's certainly some sort of ultimate in complexity. Let the reader be warned that it is more complex than Chess. This may delight Chess buffs, but I don't want to incur the wrath of those who aren't Chess players.

I've played this game for years and have taught it to a number of my friends and acquaintances, who find a challenge to their skill and imagination in what they now call — to my dismay — Abbott's Ultima. The game uses Chess pieces and the Chessboard. Since Ultima is not a card game, I at first hesitated to include it in this book. But Chess pieces are as plentiful as playing cards; and the purpose of this book is to present a group of new games that do not require special equipment. I also wanted to expose the readers of this book to a game for which my friends and I have already developed some intriguing strategies. It was our hope that if the game became more widely known, other players might contribute to its strategy and make it even more interesting than it has already proven to be to aficionados of complex games.

Introduction   CHESS PIECES are almost as adaptable to new games as playing cards are. There have been several variations on Chess that use the pieces with certain changes or additions to the rules of Chess. However, Ultima is not strictly a Chess variation, since it is an almost complete re-use of the Chess pieces. Only one of its pieces, the king, retains the same function it has in Chess. A few of the other pieces in Ultima are taken from a number of other war games.

Ultima contains elements from games that have appeared at various times throughout history. And the basic idea behind Ultima originated in some observations on the history of games. However, it is this basic idea that makes the game very different from others.

The main element that sets apart one board game, or group of board games, from another is the method of capture. There has been a great variety of these captures, some of which are no longer found in games played today. But it can be noted that each particular game uses only one form of capture. Chess, for instance, has different moves for its pieces, but each piece captures in the same fashion, by moving onto the same space as the piece it is capturing. Checkers has one form of capture, the short leap, even though the men and the kings have different powers of movement.

The question occurred as to whether it might be possible to construct a game that used, not one, but several different forms of capture. This question then became the basic concept behind the development of Ultima. Thus there are seven different pieces in Ultima, each one using a different form of capture.

Before I explain the game itself, it might be interesting to explain the sources from which the captures used are derived.

The capture performed by the king is of course the familiar replacement capture found in Chess, and it needs no explanation. Another fairly familiar capture is performed by the piece called the "long-leaper." This is a variation of the long leap of Polish and Spanish Checkers. The capture is similar to the short leap of regular Checkers except that the piece may travel any distance in a straight line before and after jumping the enemy piece.

The piece called the "withdrawer" captures by moving *away* from the enemy piece it is capturing. This is an unusual sort of capture that I have seen only in the description of a Madagascan game called Fanorona.

The pawns in Ultima use a form of the "interception" capture, which is also called the "custodian" capture in some books. A pawn captures an enemy piece when it traps the enemy in the middle between itself and another friendly piece. This capture is the one that will be least familiar to players of modern games, but it is actually the oldest form of capture found in war games. The Greeks played a game that involved this capture as far back as 500 B.C., and their game was probably taken from an older Egyptian game. In contrast, the replacement capture of the Chess games did not appear until about 600 A.D. Interception was the form of capture in the popular Roman game Latrunculi, it was used in the Saxon game Hnefatafl, and it appeared in other games throughout the world. However, with the end of the Roman Empire and with the rise of Chess, this capture disappeared entirely, so that it now seems quite strange to us. But in a sense the war games that use interception seem to be the ones that are most representative of actual warfare; one can almost picture two swordsmen taking an enemy between them.

The "coordinator" in Ultima is an original piece that captures in a way not found in other known games. The "immobilizer" is also an original piece. It does not actually capture but instead paralyzes any enemy piece it is next to. The "chameleon" does not have its own method of capture, but instead it captures an enemy piece in the manner that that enemy piece captures.

With these various forms of capture in the game, it is apparent that the rules are going to be complicated. But Ultima has the great advantage that after it is played once or twice, it becomes possible to see quite clearly what is going on. And when the game does become clear to the players, they should be able to plan their strategy for several moves ahead. There will, unfortunately, be some opportunity for sneak attack and blunders, but you should find these reduced as you gain experience, as is the case in Chess.

Preliminary

BEFORE setting up the pieces, each player should place a rubber band or piece of tape on one of his rooks or in some way mark it to distinguish it from the other rook. This marked rook is to be the immobilizer. The one that is not marked is the coordinator. The other pieces are renamed as follows: the knights are called long-leapers, the bishops are chameleons, and the queen is the withdrawer. The king is still called king, and the pawns are still pawns.

In the diagrams in these instructions the pieces are represented by the first letter of their name, except for the chameleon, which is arbitrarily designated by S to distinguish it from the coordinator, which is designated by C.

Diagram 1 shows how the pieces are set up. The pieces

C	L	S	W	K	S	L	I
P	P	P	P	P	P	P	P
P	P	P	P	P	P	P	P
I	L	S	K	W	S	L	C

Diagram 1

124

are in the same starting position as in Chess, except that the White king is on a white square instead of a black square. The pieces belonging to one player are represented by plain letters and the pieces of the other player are represented by letters enclosed in circles. In the remainder of these diagrams the plain letters will be used to represent friendly pieces and the letters in circles to represent the enemy.

A player moves one of his pieces in his turn. The player with the White pieces makes the first move, after which the turn alternates between the players. Deciding which person is to play White can be done by lot or by arrangement between the players.

The following are the moves each piece can make and the ways in which they capture.

King

THE KING can move one space in any direction, provided the space it moves onto is not occupied by a friendly piece. It captures by replacement, by moving onto a square that is occupied by an enemy piece and thus removing that piece.

The object of the game is to capture the enemy king. The players declare check in a fashion similar to that of Chess. That is, if a player makes a move that puts him in a position to take the enemy king on the next move, he announces check. A player may not move into a position that puts his own king in check.

The game is won when a player achieves checkmate, attacking the enemy king in such a way that it cannot escape capture by the next turn. A player also wins if his opponent is unable to move any of his pieces. (This is, of course, different from Chess; for when a player cannot move in Chess, the game is a draw. It is my own personal opinion that Chess itself could be improved if that rule were changed, but I expect most Chess players would argue with me about that.)

A game of Ultima is a draw when both players agree that neither can force checkmate.

Movement

BEFORE DESCRIBING the captures performed by the pieces other than the king, I must describe their powers of movement. The rules governing the *direction* these pieces move are fairly simple. The withdrawer, coordinator, immobilizer, chameleon, and long-leaper are all alike in that they can move in a straight line in any direction, orthogonally (vertically or horizontally) or diagonally. The pawns are more restricted; they can move only orthogonally, not diagonally.

The rule governing the *distance* these pieces move is more complex. How far one of them can move depends on where it is on the board. Generally, a piece will have increased mobility if it has moved into enemy territory, and, conversely, its mobility decreases if it retreats back towards its own side of the board. With the exception of the king, here is the rule governing distance: A player may move a piece on his first row only one square; he may move a piece on his second row one or two squares; he may move a piece on his third row one, two, or three squares; and so on—the fourth row up to four squares, fifth up to five, sixth up to six. And a player's piece on his seventh or eighth row has the maximum mobility; it can move from one to seven squares.

Pieces may not move onto or over squares occupied by friendly pieces, nor may they move onto or over squares occupied by enemy pieces except when those enemy are being taken by the long-leap or replacement capture.

A couple of examples should help clarify these rules of movement. The pawn in Diagram 2 could move onto any of the squares marked with a small arrow. If it moved back to the position shown in Diagram 3, it would, on the next turn, be able to move only one or two squares, as shown in that diagram.

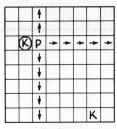

Diagram 2

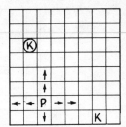

Diagram 3

The friendly withdrawer (the one uncircled) in Diagram 4 has wide-ranging mobility, as shown by the arrows. In contrast, the enemy withdrawer is only on the opponent's third row. If it were his turn to move, he could move his withdrawer only onto one of the squares shown with an arrow in Diagram 5.

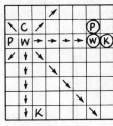

Diagram 4

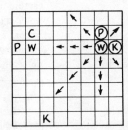

Diagram 5

Pawns

THE PAWNS use the interception form of capture. If a pawn moves onto a square that is *orthogonally* next to an enemy piece, and there is a friendly piece on the other side of that enemy piece, then the enemy piece is captured and removed from the board. As an example, if the pawn in Diagram 6 moves up to the head of the arrow, it captures the enemy withdrawer.

127

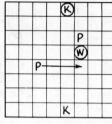

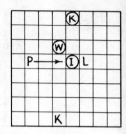

Diagram 6   Diagram 7

The stationary friendly piece that assists in the capture need not also be a pawn. For instance, the pawn in Diagram 7 captures the enemy immobilizer, since it traps the immobilizer between itself and the friendly long-leaper.

To use this form of capture, however, the piece that does the moving must be the pawn. If the long-leaper in Diagram 8 moved to the head of the arrow, it would not capture the immobilizer, even though the immobilizer would again be trapped between the pawn and the long-leaper. The piece that does the moving determines the method of capture, and the long-leaper uses an entirely different form of capture.

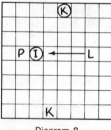

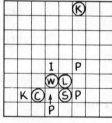

Diagram 8   Diagram 9

It is a general rule in Ultima that if a capture is to be effected it must be made by the piece that is moved, and the form of capture involved must be that of the piece that is moved. What might be considered an exception to this is the chameleon, since the chameleon captures in the manner of the piece it is capturing. Thus a chameleon might move and make a capture by interception, but only if the piece it is capturing is a pawn.

Another general rule is that a player is not required to make a capture, even if one is open to him. However, if a piece is moved so that a capture is effected, the captured piece must be removed, even though in a rare circumstance the player who made the capture might prefer to leave the enemy piece in place.

A pawn may capture more than one enemy piece in a move. If the pawn in Diagram 9 moves to the head of the arrow, it captures three enemy pieces: the withdrawer, the coordinator, and the chameleon. It does not capture the enemy long-leaper, since it has not moved to the square orthogonally next to the long-leaper.

A piece may move to the square between an enemy pawn and another enemy piece without fear of being captured by the pawn on the enemy's next turn.

Withdrawer   THE WITHDRAWER can capture a piece it is next to by moving any number of squares directly away from that piece. In other words, to make a capture it must start its move on a square that is orthogonally or diagonally next to the piece it means to capture, and it must move in a straight line directly away from that piece. A withdrawer can capture only one piece in a move.

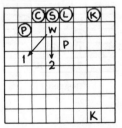

Diagram 10

In Diagram 10 the withdrawer could capture the long-leaper by moving any number of squares along arrow No. 1, or it could capture the chameleon by moving any number of squares along arrow No. 2. It cannot capture the coordinator in the diagram, since it could not move directly away from that piece. Nor can it capture the enemy pawn, because it is not on a square next to this pawn.

Long-Leaper THE LONG-LEAPER can leap over and capture an enemy piece if the first square beyond the enemy is vacant and if the long-leaper's present power of movement is sufficient to carry it at least to that first square beyond.

The long-leaper in Diagram 11 has a choice of one of two captures. It could capture the coordinator by moving either to the square numbered 1 or the square numbered 2. Or instead it could capture the immobilizer by moving either to square 3 or square 4. It could not capture any of the three enemy pawns, because there is no vacant square beyond any of the three. The first square on the other side of the withdrawer is vacant, but the long-leaper could not capture the withdrawer, because its present power of movement would not carry it to that square.

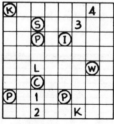

Diagram 11

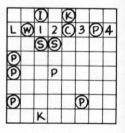

Diagram 12

The long-leaper need not stop on the first square beyond a piece it captures but can continue moving in a straight line. If another enemy piece lies on this straight line, the long-leaper may also capture it, again provided the first square beyond is vacant and provided the long-leaper can move as far as the square beyond. In this way, the long-leaper can capture up to three pieces in one move.

In Diagram 12 the long-leaper could capture the with-drawer by moving to square 1 or square 2, or it could capture both the withdrawer and the coordinator by moving to square 3, or it could capture the withdrawer, the coordinator, and a pawn by moving to square 4.

No other captures are open to the long-leaper in this diagram. After leaping the withdrawer, it could not in the same turn capture either chameleon, since this would involve a change in direction. It cannot capture any of the three enemy pawns it lies on a vertical line with, because the square beyond the first pawn it would encounter is not vacant. It cannot capture the pawn at the lower right, because it is blocked by a friendly pawn, and the long-leaper may not leap friendly pieces.

Coordinator   WHEN THE coordinator finishes a move, it captures any enemy piece that is on an intersection of the orthogonal lines that pass through the coordinator and through the friendly king.

In Diagram 13, if the coordinator moves to the head of the arrow, it captures the enemy pawn; for this pawn is on the intersection of the vertical dotted line that passes through the king, and the horizontal dotted line which passes through the point where the coordinator finished its move.

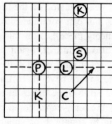

Diagram 13

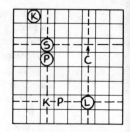

Diagram 14

A coordinator can also capture two pieces in a single move. In Diagram 14, if the coordinator moves up one space, it captures the enemy chameleon and long-leaper. The orthogonal lines that run through the king and through the coordinator at the end of its move are drawn as dotted lines in the diagram.

Most players find this method of capture the most difficult to perceive. One helpful way to look at it is to think of the squares on the Chessboard as squares on a map and the rows and columns as coordinates of the map. At the end of a move, the coordinator will be on the intersection of two of these coordinates, and the king may be on the intersection of two different coordinates. These four coordinate lines will also come together at two other squares on the board, and, if there are any enemy pieces on either of these squares, those pieces are captured.

If, when the coordinator finishes its move, it is on one of the same coordinate lines as the king, then no captures are made. This is the situation that results in Diagram 15 when the coordinator moves to the head of the arrow. Thus no capture results from this move.

A piece may move onto an intersection of the coordinate lines that pass through the enemy king and coordinator. However, in doing so, it may place itself in danger of being captured by the coordinator on the next move.

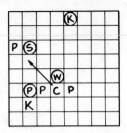

Diagram 15

Notice back in Diagram 13 that the long-leaper was on the intersection of the coordinate lines *before* as well as after the coordinator moved.

Moving the king, instead of the coordinator, does not effect a capture by the coordinator, even if an enemy piece would then be on an intersection of the coordinate lines. The general rule stated before applies here, that the form of capture must be that of the piece that is moved; and the king captures in a different fashion.

It might appear difficult to anticipate an attack from the coordinator. However, if a player watches what pieces he has on a line with the enemy king, he will be able to see which are vulnerable to attack by the coordinator.

Immobilizer   THE DREAD IMMOBILIZER does not make a capture; for it does not remove its victims from the board, but instead it paralyzes any enemy piece it is next to in an orthogonal or diagonal direction. Any enemy piece the immobilizer moves next to, or any enemy piece that moves next to the immobilizer, loses its power of movement. This power is restored, however, if the immobilizer moves away or is captured.

133

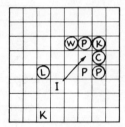

Diagram 16

In Diagram 16 the immobilizer moves to the head of the arrow and paralyzes the enemy king, withdrawer, coordinator, and two pawns. However, by this move it frees the enemy long-leaper, which had previously been immobilized. It is not necessary to announce check before immobilizing a king.

A piece may move past an enemy immobilizer without being paralyzed, but if it lands on a square next to the immobilizer, it loses its power of movement. If the two immobilizers come together, they of course immobilize each other as well as any enemy piece they remain in contact with. Neither immobilizer thus can move unless the other is captured.

The Suicide Move

A PIECE that is immobilized does have one special move it can make, that of suicide. A player may use a turn to remove from the board one of his own pieces that is immobilized. This is sometimes a valuable move since it may clear the way for an attack on the immobilizer.

A piece removed in this fashion is treated as if it had been captured and it is not returned to the board. A player may not, of course, have his king commit suicide.

134

THE FUNCTION of the chameleon can be simply stated: it does to pieces what they do to other pieces.

This does not mean that the chameleon can use any form of capture it wishes but that it must capture only in the manner of the piece it captures.

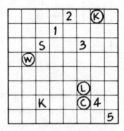

Diagram 17

In Diagram 17, if the chameleon moved to square 1 or 2 it would capture the withdrawer, since it would have withdrawn from that piece. Or instead, it could move to square 3 and capture the coordinator, for the coordinator would then be on an intersection of the orthogonal lines that run through the chameleon and through the friendly king. Or it could capture the long-leaper by leaping over it to square 4 or 5.

Whenever the chameleon is capturing a pawn, it must observe a special restriction on its movement. Since pawns may not move diagonally, the chameleon may not capture a pawn by a diagonal move. For example, the chameleon in Diagram 18 can move to the head of the arrow and capture the pawn by interception, the pawn's method of capturing. The chameleon in Diagram 19 could also move to the head of the arrow, but it would not thereby capture the pawn, since it moved diagonally.

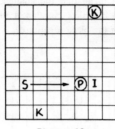

Diagram 18

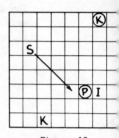

Diagram 19

Also, since a king can never move more than one square, a chameleon may not capture a king on a move of more than one square. In its present position in Diagram 20, the chameleon does not have the king in check since it is more than one square away from the king. But if it moves to the head of the arrow it does put the king in check, since on its next turn it could move one square and capture the king by replacement, the king's method of capture.

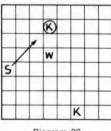

Diagram 20

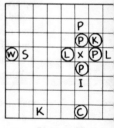

Diagram 21

A chameleon can do many things in a single move. In the unlikely situation shown in Diagram 21 the chameleon leaps over the long-leaper to the spot marked *x*. It thereby captures the long-leaper, the withdrawer, the coordinator, three pawns, and it gives check to the king.

A chameleon also can immobilize an immobilizer by moving next to it, or an immobilizer becomes paralyzed if it moves next to a chameleon. In either case both pieces become paralyzed and neither can move unless the other is captured. The immobilizer in this case continues to paralyze any other enemy piece it is next to, although the chameleon of course lacks this ability.

A chameleon cannot capture another chameleon.

Sample Game

THIS SAMPLE game, which was played by a couple of beginners, is presented only to show one way that games of Ultima can be recorded. The squares of the board are numbered as in Diagram 22. In recording the moves, the letter representing the piece moved is given first, followed by the square it moved from and the square it moved to. Following this is the letter of any enemy piece it captured and the notation *ch* if it gives check. The final position of the pieces in this game is shown in Diagram 23 (with the uncircled letters representing the white pieces).

WHITE	BLACK
Pf2-f4	Pc7-c5
We1-f2	Pb7-b5
Wf2-d4	Sc8-c7
Wd4-e3xP	Pd7-d5
We3-c5	Wd8-d7
Pa2-a4	Pa7-b7
Lb1-a2	Wd7-e6
La2-c4	Sc7-c6
Wc5-a7	Pb5-a5
Wa7-a6xC	Sc6-c3xL
Pa4-c4xS	Pb7-a7xW
Pb2-b4	Pg7-g5
Ia1-b2	Lb8-b7
Ib2-d4	Lb7-b5
Pb4-a4	Lg8-g7
Ph2-h4	Lg7-e5
Pc2-c3	Ih8-g7
Ph4-h5	Lb5-b6
Pe2-e3	Ig7-g6
Pf4-f5xP	We6-d7xP
Sf1-f2	Wd7-b5
Id4-c5	Le5-b2xP
Sf2-f4	Pe7-e5
Sf4-h6	Lb2-a3
Ic5-b4	Sf8-e7
Lg1-f2	Se7-c5
Lf2-f4	W-suicide
Lf4-b8xPch	Lb6-d8
Ch1-h2	Pf7-f8
Ch2-f4	Ld8-e7
Cf4-e5xP	Le7-g5
Ce5-d5	Lg5-e5
Pe3-e1	Le5-b2
Kd1-e2ch	Ke8-f7
Cd5-b7xL	Kf7-g7
Ke2-f3	Kg7-h6xS
Kf3-g4	Ig6-f5
Ph5-g5	Kh6-h5
	mate

a8 b8 c8 d8 e8 f8 g8 h8
a7 b7 c7 d7 e7 f7 g7 h7
a6 b6 c6 d6 e6 f6 g6 h6
a5 b5 c5 d5 e5 f5 g5 h5
a4 b4 c4 d4 e4 f4 g4 h4
a3 b3 c3 d3 e3 f3 g3 h3
a2 b2 c2 d2 e2 f2 g2 h2
a1 b1 c1 d1 e1 f1 g1 h1

Diagram 22

Diagram 23

FUNK & WAGNALLS PAPERBOOKS

THE ALDUS SHAKESPEARE

FUNK & WAGNALLS PAPERBOOKS